Money and Politics

Issues in Policy History
General Editor: Donald T. Critchlow

MONEY AND
POLITICS

Edited by
Paula Baker

The Pennsylvania State University Press
University Park, Pennsylvania

This work was originally published as a special issue of *Journal of Policy History* (vol. 14, no. 1, 2002). This is its first separate paperback publication.

Library of Congress Cataloguing-in-Publication Data

Money and politics / edited by Paula Baker.
    p. cm.—(Issues in policy history ; #9)
  Originally published as a special issue of Journal of policy history (vol. 14, no. 1, 2002). Includes bibliographical references.
  ISBN 0-271-02246-9 (pbk.)
    1. Campaign funds—United States. 2. Elections—United States. 3. Pressure groups—United States. I. Baker, Paula C. II. Journal of policy history. III. Series.

JK1991 .M7273 2002
324.7'8'0973—dc21

Contents

Editor's Preface

Although there is no biblical injunction declaring, "Ye shall have campaign finance reform with you forever," this issue, much like the poor, appears to be perennial and refuses to go away. As the authors in this volume show, campaign finance reform and the larger problem of money and politics are not new issues that emerged in the late twentieth century, but are problems that date to the early Republic and the emergence of mass democratic politics.

Indeed, a strong case can be made that the issue of special interests, privilege, and politics—and the calls for reform—lays at the core of the American Revolution. Accusations of undue moneyed influence were heard time and again as the American nation took shape. Most notably was the controversy over the chartering of the United States Second Bank in 1816 (the first having been established in 1791 with great contention) that led to charges by the bank's detractors of powerful financial forces at work in promoting the bank. When the bank came up for rechartering in 1832, Jackson vetoed legislation to renew the bank's charter, declaring, "The rich and powerful too often bend the acts of government to their selfish purposes." He suggested that those members of Congress who had voted for the rechartering of the Second Bank had been unduly influenced by "our rich men [and British bankers]" who "have not been content with equal protections and benefits."

While the essays in this volume clearly reveal the long history and varying contexts that the general issue of money and politics, and the subordinate problem of campaign finance reform, has played in American politics, the exact influence of financial contributions to candidates and incumbents on public policy remains, as Professor Baker observes, considerably more ambiguous. Money (unless it is an outright bribe) does not buy votes. On the other hand, large contributors contribute money to candidates—often two rival candidates—in order to buy access. Yet in a democracy, even the appearance of wealthy contributors gaining greater access to politicians has stirred protest and has led Congress to enact numerous regulations to limit influence. As a consequence, Congress in the twentieth century has undertaken many attempts at campaign reform. In 1925, the Corrupt Practices Act consolidated federal law to address the issue of campaign finance by requiring campaign treasurers to report all contributions of $100 or more and placing limits on candidate expenditures. The Federal Election Campaign Act (FECA) of 1971 returned to the issue of federal campaign finances, establishing parameters on campaign spending and barring direct contributions from corporations and unions. FECA was amended in 1974 to further define campaign finance reform and to create the Federal Election Commission to administer and oversee campaign law. A series of constitutional decisions, *Buckley v. Valeo* (1976), *Communication Workers of America v. Beck* (1988), and *Colorado Republican Federal Campaign Committee v. Federal Election Committee* (1998), further clarified the 1974 legislation.

In the 1990s, campaign finance reform once again came into prominence. Senator John McCain (R-Ariz.) and Senator Russell Feingold (D-Wis.) proposed the Bipartisan Campaign Reform Act of 1997, only to find a Senate filibuster barring the bill from coming to a vote. The bill was reintroduced in 1999, passed the House, but again failed to reach a Senate vote. Senator McCain placed campaign reform as a centerpiece in his campaign for the Republican party presidential nomination. Although McCain failed to get the Republican nomination, campaign finance reform was far from dead. The average amount of money raised in Senate, House, and Presidential campaigns in 2000 reached the astronomical figure of $2.2 billion.

Encouraged by public sentiment against the cost of elections, Senators McCain and Feingold and Representative Christopher Shays (R-Conn.) submitted the same Bipartisan Campaign Finance Reform Bill to Congress in June 2001. Nine months later the bill passed the Republican-controlled House and the Democratic-controlled Congress. President George W. Bush signed it into law on March 27, 2002. That same day, the National Rifle Association (NRA) and Senator Mitch McConnell (R-Ky.) filed separate suits challenging the law's prohibition of soft-money contributions from independent organizations for political advertising three months before an election.

In this volume, Professor Baker has assembled a distinguished group of scholars to place money and politics in a broad historical context. These essays show how the concerns of policymakers have changed over time, but moreover, these essays reveal how integral money has been to the rise of mass democracy in the United States. That money fostered the growth of democracy—yet potentially threatened to corrupt democracy itself—presents, as Professor Baker observes, one of the great paradoxes of American politics.

Donald T. Critchlow
General Series Editor

PAULA BAKER

Introduction: Does Money Buy Policy?

Money in politics is a funny thing. By legend and cliché, money is the "mother's milk of politics," that which keeps party machinery working and campaigns running. It is also the focus of generations of suspicion and complaint. From the advent of the "spoils system" in the early nineteenth century to the PACs and "soft money" of today, there appear to be few takers for the proposition that money does not stain what ought to be the majesty and purity of politics. Money, unlike the suffrage, introduces inequality among citizens. Money gives its favored candidates and policies an unfair advantage for the public's attention. Money is the appearance, if not the fact, of corruption.

Such sentiments may be widely yet lightly held. Only on rare occasions—perhaps during the early twentieth-century furor over the connections between business and politics—has the matter of money and politics seemed to ascend fairly high on the scale of public priorities. Rather, it is an issue that has animated people in or near the political action. Even then, it has usually taken dramatic events—President James Garfield's assassination and Watergate, for example—to bring reforms into focus. For the wider public, the idea that money has too large a role in American politics rests alongside the sense that there are more important issues.

In this historians perhaps mirror public sentiment. While campaign finance has been a fairly consistent interest of political scientists, few historians have given the subject sustained attention. Matthew Josephson told lurid stories about the venality and greed of late nineteenth-century politicians (which Mark Walgren Summers, in this issue and elsewhere, places in a more realistic light); tales of Mark Hanna's fund-raising wizardry are a standard feature of accounts of the election of 1896. Campaign finance merits some discussion in a great number of accounts of elections and politicians, but Clifton K. Yearley's 1970 *The Money Machines* stands out as a sustained treatment of the subject.[1]

Still, there are signs of growing interest in the history of campaign finance, and that history ought to be of interest to policy historians. A few questions emerge immediately. Does money buy policy in a direct way? Studies of contemporary legislators cast doubt on the idea of systemic influence. The essays in this collection suggest that historically, too, a few politicians may have been on the take, but that selling policy to the highest bidder was not standard procedure. Some early nineteenth-century legislators worried about the corrupting power of patronage and, to a lesser extent, assessments of government workers (though not enough of them did so to block the practices). Later in the nineteenth century, newspaper editors retold wild stories about the wealth of the opposition, but party leaders got wealthy benefactors to open their wallets with difficulty. And then, their luck was best with businessmen who already supported the party's program. The Franklin Roosevelt 1936 campaign rejected contributions aimed at lessening labor's influence on the Democratic party.[2]

It is nonetheless hard to put aside the assumption that large amounts of money must somehow have a loud voice. If nothing else, the time it takes to raise money must have some impact—perhaps in dissuading good people from running for office; perhaps in taking unpopular positions. Democrats and Republicans alike in the 1960s and 1970s decried the amount of money they needed to raise and the time they had to spend raising it—time that otherwise, presumably, would go to the public's work. Nineteenth-century candidates, Summers points out, also needed to pay their share to their party's coffers. Earlier in the century, personal wealth seemed perhaps even more important to a political career. How the fund-raising barrier to entry to a political career stacks up against others—say, a willingness to campaign and seem to get nowhere near the respect deserved—remains unclear.

To put the money and political influence question another way, has reform made a difference in the kind of politics or policy we get? Have voters been wise to put issues (or character) above process questions like campaign finance in their hierarchy of concerns?

History can add perspective to the contemporary debate about campaign finance. We might learn not merely that money has always had a place in American politics, but that the kinds of concerns that policymakers had changed through time. Robert Mutch's essay, on the debate about patronage and assessments in the 1830s, suggests how old frameworks—in this case seventeenth-century concerns about corruption—framed politicians' responses to new developments. Mark Walgren Summers highlights new information on financing Gilded Age campaigns that deflates the routine charges about businessmen and their corrupt political cronies. By analyzing the uses and sources of funds, however, he also provides a fascinating account of how late nineteenth-century politics worked. My essay looks at two cases, the 1868 Republican presidential campaign and the 1954 California gubernatorial race, to illustrate how fundraising along with raising a workforce can tell us about changes in the ways campaigns try to connect with voters. What can campaign finance reform, Julian Zelizer asks—efforts that began well before the Watergate scandal—tell us about Americans' cynicism about politics and government? He also points out that campaign finance reform works as a case study of policymaking: a case where policy entrepreneurs without substantial backing from either politicians or an outraged public shaped the debate.

The history of campaign finance seems to leave us with a puzzle. As these essays taken together illustrate that since the rise of mass parties, raising money has also raised controversy—money would seem to potentially corrupt democracy. Yet the question arose when mass parties, in contrast to the earlier clusters of elites, pulled men below the moneyed classes into political office. The loudest complaints about systems of fundraising have come from politicians and their allies themselves, often for partisan purposes, and from relatively elite groups, such as academics and political commentators. History may not indicate what method of fund-raising might fit best with democratic participation, but it can alert us to some of the pitfalls of reform.

Notes

1. Matthew Josephson, *The Politicos* (New York, 1938); Clifton K. Yearley, *The Money Machines: The Breakdown and Reform of Governmental and Party Finance in the North, 1860–1920* (Albany, N.Y., 1970). Representative of an older tradition in political science are Louise Overacker, *Money in Elections* (New York, 1932); and Alexander Heard, *The Costs of Democracy* (Chapel Hill, N.C., 1960).

2. Among others, Randall Barrow, John M. Duncan, Emmet D. Hehn, and William Bendle to Stephen Early (wire), 26 January 1937; and Early to Theodore Kingsbury, 28 January 1937, Official File, Papers of Franklin D. Roosevelt, Democratic National Committee, Franklin D. Roosevelt Library. The president's office could not accept such personal contributions, but those without an antilabor message received a supportive response and instructions to send the contribution to the DNC offices in New York.

PAULA BAKER

Campaigns and Potato Chips;
or Some Causes and Consequences
of Political Spending

Before getting too upset about the initially eye-popping sums candidates spend to win elections, law professor (and current member of
the Federal Election Commission) Bradley A. Smith advises us to
put campaign costs in perspective. Americans, he notes, spent two
or three times more on potato chips than on electing candidates in
the mid-1990s. For Smith, the potato chip example is only one illus-
tration that ought to settle fears about "obscene" and "runaway" campaign expenses. Perspective, however, is unlikely to move those
convinced that big donors drive the political agenda. Convinced
that money and politics is a far more nefarious combination than fat
and salt, campaign finance reformers will no doubt carry on their
search for new ways to limit spending and contributions, continuing
the Progressive Era crusade to eliminate money's degrading influence on democracy.[1]

Commissioner Smith's comparison suggests a way of approaching the "problem" of money in politics that sets aside the matter of
morality. What would we learn if we literally considered campaigns
as a business, like snack foods, package delivery, or transportation?
Campaigns face organizational problems that are common to industry. Like all businesses, they must raise capital, assemble a labor force,
identify products, arrive at a marketing plan and pitch, determine
which tasks to keep internally and which to purchase from the outside, maintain a flow of good information within the organization,
and coordinate the work of various layers of the "firm." Like many
businesses, campaigns have dealt with increasing levels of federal
and state regulation. Like greeting cards, campaigns are largely sea-
sonal businesses; the political calendar of issues and elections, however, can keep operations running much of the time. Like all
purveyors of consumer goods and services, campaigns must grab the

attention of a distracted public. Measuring how well they are doing that has changed with available technologies, but in contrast to most industries, political campaigns produce winners and losers on a date certain. But just as business school case studies pick apart firms' decisions, explaining election results can occupy strategists, pundits, and scholars who hope to avoid mistakes, to capitalize on successes, or simply to understand.[2]

In business terms, political history has typically focused on the pitch and product—issues and candidates—as well as consumer, or voter, behavior. This essay is a pass at the business of campaigns as a whole, from raising capital and a workforce through measuring effectiveness and solving communication and coordination problems. It takes two Republican cases, widely separated in time: the presidential election of 1868 and the California gubernatorial election in 1954.[3] Each illustrates how parties and candidates overcame difficulties—in building a national organization in the first case, and in running campaigns without benefit of party coordination in the second. Each points to how innovations in raising funds and running campaigns would have significant political consequences that went well beyond the November result. Treating politics as an industry can help us see why reform of campaigns and spending has fallen well short on the promise of politics dedicated to the "public interest."[4]

Republican prospects in 1868 were as good as any reasonable partisan might hope. Heading the ticket was General Ulysses S. Grant, nominated unanimously on the first ballot at the May convention. His brief acceptance letter opened a campaign in which he said even less. "Let us have peace," Grant wrote in closing his letter, and his supporters gladly filled in the meanings of his silence, his military fame, and his indifferent Democratic loyalties in the 1850s. Some imagined a president compliant with congressional plans for Reconstruction; others a strong, honest leader; others still a moderate peacemaker who could find the right formula for the defeated South. The electoral map, as well as the luster at the top of the ticket, made Republicans like their chances. No serious factional battles disturbed the party's base in New England and the upper Midwest. The Reconstruction Acts of 1867 had removed the Southern pro-Confederate state governments, provided military oversight, and set the stage for "loyal" governments to be formed in the South. The votes of African Americans, northern newcomers, and Unionist whites, absent election-day fraud and violence, could turn the former Confederacy Republican.

The Democrats' July meeting in New York, by contrast, had no shortage of candidates or contention. The convention gathered together Tammany Hall politicians, a sprinkling of old Eastern wealth, the founder of the Ku Klux Klan, and Midwestern Copperhead luminaries. Southerners and Westerners, their regions burdened by credit problems and debt, sought a candidate who would support easy money policies; Easterners sought the most rapid return as possible to the prewar monetary footing. Democrats turned to Horatio Seymour, a former governor of New York and hard money man who nonetheless had few dedicated enemies in the party. Seymour would not prove to be an electrifying candidate, but Democrats needed neither a rallying point nor a definition of what they were for: they knew what they were against. They sought the end of military Reconstruction and all that congressional Reconstruction meant—the threat of racial equality, the expansion of the federal government, the pile of national debt, and onerous taxes to pay for the misguided schemes. They also knew how tenuous Republican unity was, especially on the question of the capabilities and talents of freedpeople as citizens. Even white Radicals, after all, had their doubts about racial equality.[5]

The Democrats, moreover, were organized everywhere in the nation. Even in the midst of war, the party had contested elections in the North, and its urban base made election day outcomes in the band of states from New York to Indiana doubtful. The party grew in the old fashioned way—built by local activists from the election district up. The "monster rallies," inevitably "splendidly attended," as party editors described them, owed to hard work and a bit of cash, not some spontaneous outpouring of partisan emotion. The editors and correspondents who wrote the stories tried to encourage enthusiasm and provide feedback on conditions to candidates and party leaders. Postmasters and others with wide public contacts also passed on local intelligence. The speakers at the rallies might have been national figures if the election was likely to be close; local talent provided the introductions and honed their skills if famous speakers could not appear. District leaders formed clubs that brought costumed, torch-carrying marchers into line. Election preparations absorbed the local leaders as well as the more active participants—canvassing voters in doubtful districts, printing and assembling the ballots, getting people to the polls, and serving as election clerks and poll watchers.

This was the party workforce. The labor pool consisted of pub-lic officials, government employees, those who hoped to land a posi-tion, and enthusiasts. Workers often hoped for personal as well as political rewards somewhere down the line, if not immediately. Edi-tors angled for influence in party circles, and, perhaps, state print-ing contracts or a patronage job if weary of the grind of publishing a marginal sheet. Speakers with national reputations laid in favors to be returned. Local talent mentioned campaign exertions when ap-plying for postmasterships or other positions. Even marchers used their willingness to parade as a claim on government largess. On election days, poll workers expected to be paid for their time; some-times, voters themselves expected payment.

Money for campaign expenses came from assessments on city, state, and federal government employees and contributions from elected officials, candidates, and a few wealthy financial angels. If the "spoils system" of appointments to federal positions came into wide use under President Andrew Jackson, by the 1850s administra-tions worked public payrollers hard. Control over national patron-age—from the employee-rich (and graft-worthy) ports of New York and Philadelphia to Interior and Treasury agents to small-town postmasterships—meant a stock of dependable election workers, sources of campaign intelligence, reliable allies at party conventions, and a great many salaries to tax. Supplying early money for cam-paigns, federal workers could expect assessment "circulars" in their mail. State parties tapped their own workers and federal employees who held assignments within their borders.[6]

Coordinating fund-raising and workers was traditionally a hap-hazard business. Both the Democratic and Republican parties had national committees, but party operations mostly fell to the state and local parties. With their own base of financial support, be it from rich candidates and individuals or assessments, state leaders knew that the national party needed them more than they needed national organization. Local ownership of parties drifted down to county leaders and below: they did the campaign work and provided information, which they saw as valuable to any politician. Parties were national in scope, but they lagged well behind the railroads in setting up centralized procedures.[7]

Building the party in the 1850s gave the Republicans more re-cent experience with piecing together a new organization than the Democrats had. What system they developed, however, existed in the North. It had not even bothered to field a ticket in parts of the

South in 1860; by 1868 it still had minimal infrastructure in place there. Republicans needed newspapers, organization from the state to election district levels, a corps of reliable workers, and a network for gathering accurate information. There were materials at hand—federal employees in the South, white Southerners who never had sympathy with the Confederacy, Northern Republican carpetbaggers, recently freed blacks, and in some states, an established free black population. The Union League had assisted African Americans to organize in 1867. But the South needed to be organized quickly, even as Republicans, North and South, disagreed about such fundamentals as the place, if any, of African Americans in the party's leadership. The party had to do this while also giving due attention to the early and competitive states of the North.[8]

Two groups, the Republican National Committee (RNC) and the Union Republican Congressional Committee (URCC), managed the project in 1868. Congressmen had formed the URCC (later the Republican National Congressional Committee) in 1860s to aid congressional candidates and support national campaigns. In 1868, it raised funds and published and distributed campaign material. According to an 1882 government brief before the Supreme Court, the URCC "perfected" a system for assessing government workers in the 1860s. It sent a circular that asked for a "voluntary" contribution in the range of 2 percent (up to 4 percent in 1868) of salary to everyone listed in the Federal Register. The RNC raised money as well, and also coordinated the assignment of national speakers and distributed money to state campaigns.[9]

The campaign plan mixed national and state resources to maximize the party's assets. At a July 9 meeting, the RNC's executive committee hoped to follow tradition in leaving most states largely to fend for themselves. These states would do so while scrambling for funds, perhaps, since the URCC would collect the assessments from all federal employees, even those based outside Washington. The RNC would coordinate speakers and distribute literature across the nation. It aimed to raise $430,000, with $350,000 drawn from states that were safe for the Republicans, wealthy, or both—New York, Massachusetts, and Pennsylvania—with Vermont, Rhode Island, Ohio, and Michigan filling in the remainder. Regional party representatives would collect contributions and develop sources of their own.[10]

National funds went to national priorities. Some of the money recognized key constituencies—the Soldiers and Sailors Committee was promised $2,000, while the purchase of two thousand copies of the *Irish Republic* was a gesture of attention to a strongly Democratic group. The RNC assumed that some states with September or October elections required outside help: both Maine and Indiana were in line for $10,000 if the state parties raised double that amount. No one expected Southern organizations—poor, fledging groups in an impoverished region—to come up with matching funds. The committee proposed to send $1,000 immediately to state organizations "with which to commence their campaign." As the season progressed, "the Committee will endeavor, if possible, to furnish them with further funds during the campaign, hoping to make the whole amount of assistance equal to one thousand dollars for each Congressional District." The RNC wrote off border states where Republicans had no chance—county committees might get literature and badges, but nothing more.[11]

The plan was as much dream as blueprint. It would not appear that the RNC had ever raised such a sum before. Everyone knew the Indiana race would be close, nasty, and expensive, but elsewhere the unexpected was sure to revise the situation and needs. Judging from the correspondence, the RNC chairman, William Claflin, gave day-to-day affairs limited attention, and Grant none at all. RNC secretary William Eaton Chandler, in close contact with Thomas L. Tullock, his counterpart at the URCC, responded to the flow of events.

Chandler, just over thirty years old but with a career in Republican politics that went back to the John C. Frémont candidacy, was an early campaign management specialist. With a team that included two other partisans, he had meticulously managed New Hampshire races. After a short career in the New Hampshire legislature, the trim, sharp-featured Chandler filled two assistant secretaryships in the Lincoln administration. When he became secretary of the RNC in 1868, he brought a knack and love for organization to the three-room headquarters at New York's Fifth Avenue Hotel. Chandler kept his eye on the national electoral map, cultivated fund-raising contacts, maintained a wide and deep network in the party, and winnowed out good information from bad. He was a new type of political operative. He eventually went on to the Senate, but for the moment he traded not so much on his attachment to a politician or financial connections but on his talent for making organizations run better than they had.[12]

Gathering accurate information took up much of Chandler's time. The basic source was his extensive correspondence with activists at all levels. Letters had their limitations. A would-be swindler who knew the system guessed that communication was slow and uncertain. He mailed out bogus "assessment circulars" to federal employees and waited for the contributions before he was arrested. Some overstated demands could still be impossible to dismiss. Neither Chandler nor Claflin believed that Congressman James G. Blaine would have trouble with his own reelection in Maine or that the state was anything but safe for the party. Still, the size of the majority in the September election mattered because the contest came so early. Blaine's stack of frantic telegrams with their gloomy predictions forced the national party to help. Maine would get most of the support it asked for in speakers, literature, and funds. Blaine was a popular figure who worked hard for the party and could persuasively make the case that a big Maine majority provided momentum going into the October and November contests.[13]

No fancy persuasion had to be used for Chandler to see Indiana as a top national priority. Indiana Republicans seemed to believe their state was the only priority. Closely divided between the parties, the state held elections in October, which meant that it both signaled and shaped what November would bring across the nation. Republicans there requested the usual things a hotly competitive state wanted—a lot of literature and well-known speakers, especially the much-in-demand men who could address German audiences in their own language. They also generated extravagant claims on the party coffers well beyond the budgeted $10,000. In late August, A. H. Conner, the state party chairman, thought he needed $50,000 from national sources; by early September, his estimate leapt to $60,000 to $75,000. Without such support, they could not combat a widely rumored (among Republicans, anyway) Democratic fraud: a scheme backed by up to $50,000 raised in Louisville alone to colonize Indiana with Kentucky Democrats. Gubernatorial candidate Conrad Baker suggested that funds for "a well organized secret police" and "a most thorough Canvass" were vital to thwarting the would-be colonists.[14]

Indiana politicians spoke almost as one on their need for more of everything, but they disagreed over where it should go. The state committee sought to centralize finances in its hands. That alarmed congressional candidates who had counted on direct support for their districts. "'Blessed are those who expect nothing for they shall not

be disappointed,'" wrote one as he described his increasingly desperate condition. Another congressional candidate thought that at the
very least the RNC should notify the entire Indiana state committee when it provided funds, "as a precaution against misuse and em-
bezzlement . . . and to prevent complaints based upon the mere
suspicion of such conduct.[15]

The RNC sorted through the Indiana mess. Chandler consulted
Indiana Senator Oliver P. Morton and set up a meeting with Chairman Conner. The meeting appeared to settle some matters. There
would be more help, $25,000 at first, most going to the state organi-
zation, but with $1,000 to $500 given to each congressional district.
Midwestern Republican party representative, U. S. Marshall, and
fund-raiser J. Russell Jones monitored spending. In the end, Chandler indicated that $35,000 went to Indiana from the RNC, with
$7,500 more from Jones's Midwestern division. If that was not
enough, "then I never did good work in my life & never will again,"
he wrote in exasperation. Although the GOP carried the state, the
funds fell far short according to (losing) congressional candidate D.
W. Voyles. "You doubted the statement we made about the amount
of money at the command of the democratic party of our state," he
wrote. "[T]his you probably regard as mere pretext upon which to
extort money from your Committee." But Democrats had "not a cent
less than $200,000," at least some of which, he implied, went to
purchase votes. Conner's end-of-election tally showed $50,000 from
national sources and lingering sour feelings over what he saw as dis-
respect for his management and effort.[16]

The need for national funds and organization was even greater
in the South. Southern party leaders were mostly optimistic about
the campaign at first. States that approved new constitutions in the
wake of the Reconstruction Acts in time (Virginia, Mississippi, and
Texas would not) were eligible for national representation. Although
into the fall it was still not clear that Alabama and Florida would
hold elections (the former would but the latter would not), Arkansas, Georgia, Louisiana, North Carolina, South Carolina, and Tennessee would be in play. Despite violent incidents and Democratic
protests, the votes on the constitutions had gone well enough to
suggest that with national contributions added to local resources,
much of the South would go to Grant.[17]

The RNC opened with the original plan, sending relatively
meager (compared to Indiana at least) thousand-dollar contributions
to state party committees. The National Union League was also in

the field working on voter registration and organization. With the RNC's and URCC's effort to centralize some aspects of fund-raising, this group, too, would seek aid. The early needs in the South were basic: canvassing voters, building local organizations, and forming campaign clubs. There were calls for "good speakers, white and colored" for rallies to combat Democratic "barbecues and public entertainments" aimed at African Americans. Editors and would-be editors called for funds to support struggling newspapers and campaign sheets.[18]

State parties set about canvassing and organizing, and the national party sorted through requests for additional aid ("Is he *reliable?*" asked Claflin about a South Carolinian). Tullock nagged Chandler to pick up the pace in meeting Southern requests, as "they are poor and suffer for their faith." Louisiana's promised $5,000 from the RNC, for example, dribbled out: by October the state party had received only $3,500 as it geared up to hire canvassers; the rest arrived at the end of the month. Unknown (and perhaps unreliable) speakers made their pitch for expenses and fees for service. In some cases factional fights made it difficult to figure out who should get the funds when they were sent. The Georgia state party chair advised the RNC that it should not send money to the Republican governor, whom he labeled an uncertain Unionist, a perjurer, drunk, and liar. At bottom a state patronage dispute, internal backbiting in Georgia and elsewhere confused the national party enough to send an observer South to try to make sense of the situation. Intraparty divisions slowed the already deliberate pace of RNC checks.[19]

Such quarrels dovetailed with the open question of how to deal with African-American voters. Some Republicans imagined that their party, like the Whigs, might be competitive in the South with anti-Democratic white votes alone. Nothing in the strongly Democratic results in the elections held under the Johnson reconstruction plan gave any hint of support for this theory. Meanwhile, Union Leagues had cultivated black political leaders who sought recognition. In South Carolina, this made for a collision, as African Americans prepared to take the chairmanship and a share of offices, while whites were not convinced that either the state or party were ready for black leadership. "The colored element overwhelms the white element of the party to its injury," wrote a white Republican. African Americans were, he thought, "shrewd but not yet educated politically." White Republican party leaders asked whether black voters were reliable or in their poverty were ultimately beholden to Democratic landowners. Party leaders also wondered how stable—and able to weather fraud and violence—state parties build on carpetbaggers, old Unionists, and freedmen could be.[20]

Democrats knew well that any hope of victory lay with the African-American vote. "[R]ich rebels coax with one breath and threaten with the next," wrote a Republican observer. Coaxing sometimes meant spending money on rallies and "entertainments" aimed at blacks. A few Democratic editors asserted that their party was the natural friend of freedpeople. If Republicans were not willing to nominate African Americans, then Democrats encouraged them to run as independents. A Northern Republican observer in South Carolina wrote that one would "surely get four or five thousand colored votes. The Democrats urge him on. . . . The Democrats are very active and well supplied with money. They have time to stir up strife in a hundred ways."[21]

Threats—and worse—came in mounting fury as the election approached. The Ku Klux Klan and other vigilante groups were not about to let the fall elections go off as peacefully as the constitutional elections had. "Negroes are daily shot dead or wounded," in South Carolina, among them the black Republican state chairman, who was murdered while on a speaking tour. "Negroes are killed almost every day while white Republicans are threatened with abuse and maltreated," wrote the governor in September. By October, another reported "a reign of terror and violence in some parts of the state, and Republicans cannot hold meetings and discuss the questions involved in the canvass" in peace. In Louisiana, perhaps as many as two hundred blacks were murdered by rioting whites. South Carolina organized a state police force to try to stop the violence, but that was a step that was beyond the means or political will in other states; the federal government would also move slowly.[22]

Democrats carried by a 2 to 1 majority Georgia and Louisiana, where intimidation and violence were rampant and Republican party leaders reluctantly advised African Americans not to go to the polls. Democrats also won big in Missouri, Tennessee, Kentucky, and Maryland—border states unaffected by congressional Reconstruction. Republicans carried the rest of the South, but except for the nearly 58 percent in South Carolina, by nothing near a landslide. Republicans lost New York, and their victories in Connecticut, Indiana, New Jersey, Ohio, and Pennsylvania were uncomfortably close. Only the New England and upper Midwestern states were truly safe. Grant had won all but eight states and a substantial 214 to 80 lead in the electoral college. But by gaining only 53 percent of the popular vote—this for a widely admired candidate and largely unified party against a dull opponent—Republicans had to wonder about the party's future course. A national strategy had produced a national victory, but one that raised as many questions as it answered.

The South and how to finance a national effort remained perhaps the most pressing of these. The national Republican party spent at least $25,000 on the southern campaigns—paltry perhaps, given the region's needs and poverty.[23] Yet, this was perhaps the best possible effort that both political and financial circumstances permitted. Congressional Reconstruction had created Republican opportunities in the South—in light of the size of the African-American population, South Carolina and Louisiana might have been as Republican as Maine, given fair elections. That was the problem. Publicizing Southern brutality might inspire Northern revulsion against the unrepentant Rebels for a time. Still, a stringent Southern policy, if that meant taking steps toward racial equality and a federal presence with no certain end, was a taste many Northerners had not acquired. The extent of the Democratic vote outside of New England and the upper Midwest was alarming. Northern voters could not be taken for granted in pursuit of the South.

The 1868 election had produced no easy course of action the party might follow. Even after the complete end of military Reconstruction (and the lesson that it was only with close monitoring of elections that the party stood a chance), the party tried out various Southern strategies. It tried supporting biracial organizations, state parties that shut out African Americans, and renegade Democrats who broke with Conservatives over state economic issues. Nothing worked. Viable state parties could not be built by spending during election years and federal patronage.[24]

As the disfranchisement of African Americans left a few pockets of Republican support in the South and as the realignment of 1896 gave the party a sturdy national majority until the 1930s, Southern Republican organizations came to life mainly for appearances at national conventions. The New Deal realignment and Republican's loss of federal patronage and power accelerated the decay. By late 1940s, a Virginia state chairman was reduced to subterfuge in raising money: in order to tap wealthy conservatives, he assured them that their contributions would not go to the rotted state party, but instead to the national ticket. He needed the contributions to fill the state's quota to the RNC. More than that, he saw southern Democrats unhappy with the drift of the New Deal and Fair Deal. The Republican party could be lifted out of its also-ran, me-too doldrums by incorporating discontented Southerners: they could be the base of a conservative party that voters there would gladly support.[25]

In 1868, however, Republican party leaders considered what they might do about the South within the limits of the funds they could raise. Indiana had been a drain, but spending there, all agreed, was unavoidable. Claims outside of that state and the South seemed, to their authors, to be just as pressing. Things in their areas were piteously rotten, they typically claimed, although reasonably well organized under the circumstances; an infusion of cash or good speakers could foil the well-funded Democrats and produce a larger Republican vote than in the previous election. Ohio, which party leaders thought would be a contributor, not a beggar, appealed for financial assistance. "[A] few dollars in money, might be expended to [great] advantage in the 12th District of Ohio," read one among numerous pleas. The Soldiers & Sailors, perhaps in a dry run for the Grand Army of the Republic's future as a runaway success in attracting national largess, got at least $1,000 more than the RNC had budgeted. States that the party did not think were worth national support, such as Delaware, received some cash in late fall, perhaps to maintain morale. By that time even wealthy states looked for help with incidental expenses, such as a transportation fund for New Yorkers who worked elsewhere but wished to vote at home. Rumors of Republican wealth and the concentration of assessment income in national coffers had perhaps created demand, but in any event requests for assistance outstripped ready cash.[26]

Worse, the Republican financial strategy brought yelps from states the RNC thought should take care of themselves without the assessments of federal workers. In July, a Wisconsin party leader lamented the state party's "willing hearts, but empty pockets," while noting the campaign's difficulties—"a desperate foe to contend with, and hosts of new foreigners to look after." "Our State Committee desires and *needs* all the money that can be raised from Federal officers," he wrote. "Give us our own officers, and men, to draw from—without calling on them to pay anything to the National Committee . . . and we will remove all doubt. The older and richer states must be looked to for funds to be used in the South and elsewhere; but we want to 'be let alone.'" The Illinois state central committee wanted RNC funds since if J. Russell Jones "had not sent the money . . .

raised here, to [Indiana] they would have no difficulty in getting what funds they needed." The states gave grudgingly of "their" federal dollars.[27]

With mounting costs, the GOP squeezed its sources for funds more tightly than they had anticipated. From summer through fall, Tullock, Chandler, and Claflin monitored the pace of assessments. Not much could be raised around Chicago, Jones believed, until after July 4, when "the people get a little warmed up." Claflin reported that assessments were going well in New England by the end of July, but elsewhere "subscriptions" appeared to be moving slowly. In September, Tullock continued to work on assessments, but thought that they might have gotten "all we can possibly derive from that source to enable us to vigorously prosecute our work." He carried on dunning "dilatory officials" in New York. In late October, he wrote that while some were "just beginning to respond" to this round of assessments, "[w]e do not expect a large sum from that source." About a week later he concluded that, "We are receiving many responses to our calls on the Departments. Small contributions generally."[28]

While at least one government worker subscribed his *"mite"* "cheerfully," to advance "the sacred cause," the assessed were not always so chipper come tax time. Some federal employees—Republicans in good standing—paid less than the circular asked or nothing at all: they felt they had already contributed their fair measure of money, time, and labor to the cause in their states or cities. Ivers Phillips, a U.S. Internal Revenue agent in Massachusetts, also donated frequently, but he asked that justice guide assessments. He resented his $200 request, since others who made as much were asked for less and a worker who made twice as much was taxed at the same amount. "It seems to me . . . that there is something wrong somewhere. . . . I want to pay my full share in proportion to others." He paid, even though his assessment was "from 95 to 100 percent higher in proportion to what received than any other that I know of in this state." Still, he assumed that the August circular would not be the last and that the URCC had a ready fix. "[M]ore money will be wanted and if so allow me to suggest the propriety of making a reassessment to equalize matters," he offered.[29]

Government workers, even including wealthy appointees in the consular service, could hardly foot the bill alone. Daniel Sickles, the flamboyant Union general later elected to Congress, who headed a New York bank in 1868, had a suggestion: RNC leaders should go directly to all national bank presidents and remind them that some

Democrats held heretical financial ideas, which made the Republicans their safe choice. Attracting these substantial contributions, however, did not rise to the level of system that Sickles had in mind until 1884. Meanwhile, well-off politicians, such as Edwin D. Morgan, Elihu Washburne, and Claflin himself gave generously to the national party effort. Moses Grinnell, active in politics since his days in the Whig party and president of the New York Chamber of Commerce and a New York bank, gave heavily. He also arranged meetings on Wall Street that produced subscriptions from New York merchants and bankers, including Hamilton Fish, John T. Stewart, Daniel Drew, Frederick A. Conkling, and Simeon B. Chittenden. Claflin raised money among his Boston associates. Jay Cooke, a friend of Chandler's, gave early and frequently. Tom A. Scott provided transportation, and the Union Pacific was also represented in the party's take. A sprinkling of manufacturers contributed, but most of the larger sums listed in the RNC correspondence came through men with mercantile, railroad, and banking connections and friendly ties to GOP leaders.[30]

"The rest of the fight is easy," Chandler reported to Grant after the Pennsylvania and Indiana elections. "Heretofore there has been some holding back; there has been too little money given us, although our true friends have been very liberal. . . . Now . . . we shall get plenty of money—*sometimes in twenty thousand lumps!*" Yet, judging from his correspondence, Chandler may have spoken too soon. Giving appeared to have slacked off once the early elections presaged victory. Donors wanted a win, it seems, not enhanced influence, although some were rewarded. Grant offered Stewart the Treasury Department post; when he could not take it, the job went to Fish. Jay followed legislation important to his interests. Jones moved from Chicago to the consular position in Brussels. Grinnell became Collector of the Port of New York, a premier position for the national party, the state machine, and to the city's merchants. His exertions for the RNC and solicitude toward city businessmen did not prevent him from losing the position in a tug of war with the state Republican organization.[31]

Chandler later recalled that in 1868 he wound up with less than half of what the RNC had planned to collect—about $200,000— although surviving sources do not allow corroboration. In 1868, the GOP, like the charities and railroads in this period, tried to introduce system and rationality into previously haphazard work. It succeeded partially, as the chaos of unplanned expenses showed, but

Chandler kept at the task. "I am a fool for going into this campaign," Chandler wrote in 1872, "but I love my party and cannot help working for it." As head of the URCC and secretary of the RNC during Grant's reelection campaign, he oversaw assessments and other fund-raising activities, which went on as they had in 1868 despite the state parties' complaints. He again singled out for spending the neediest cases—some Southern states, Pennsylvania, Maine, and Indiana. He tried to shrug off most other claimants by repeating that the national offices only organized and paid speakers and provided literature.[32]

More important in the long run, RNC fund-raising in 1868 fired controversy about campaign finance. Ongoing attacks on the assessment of government workers and the entire patronage system of which it was part soon became more than just a hobby of some Northeastern elites. Civil servants, especially the growing ranks of professionals, grumbled about the indignities of patronage and the tax system that targeted them. The extent and insistence of assessments, as well as the amount of time civil servants spent on political work was fodder for the reform press. By 1872, Liberal Republicans, decrying the corruption within Grant's administration and arguing for civil service reform, bolted the party. President Grant responded to criticism by promising reform and creating a civil service commission; Republican presidential candidates who immediately followed him denounced the use of money gained by assessments in campaigns. Hayes, by executive order, barred the practice in 1877. With the passage of the Pendelton Act in 1883 (and similar legislation in some states), groups of government jobs slowly moved out of the patronage system and into one of appointments by examination with dismissal for cause.[33]

Yet, it was not so easy to walk away from the campaign labor of government workers and their assessment dollars. Postmasters and other government workers with wide contacts continued into the twentieth century to provide campaign intelligence, to distribute literature, to work for candidates, and to contribute toward their party's success. Fear that the New Deal's vast new national network of relief and social service workers and recipients would become a political workforce that Chandler could only dream of inspired the 1939 Hatch Act, which further curbed the political activities of government employees. Public employees' dollars, paid voluntarily or not, persisted at the state level, and in a small way at the national level into the twentieth century. But just as the contributions of government workers became trickier to access, the growth of industrial corporations opened new fund-raising opportunities. "Fat frying"—working industrialists who might be interested in high tariff rates for their products—and "strike bills," threatened regulatory measures that might be stopped through a timely contribution, were fund-raising techniques bordering on extortion that have gone down in lore of Gilded Age politics. More decorous methods, such as regular party and corporate relationships cemented by the place of politicians on corporate boards, became more common by the 1890s.[34]

Business contributions soon became, if anything, more loudly denounced than assessments had been. Government contractors, no doubt, aimed to maintain their lucrative relationships, although the classic Gilded Age financial scandals had to do with payoffs to individual legislators rather than with campaign contributions. Some industrialists fought off regulations and tariff tinkering that might harm their industries. But except perhaps when driven by fear, as in the 1896 McKinley/Bryan campaign, the chance to write checks to parties or candidates was not one that most businessmen were likely to seek. Still, the real or apparent illicit connections between business and politics fueled Progressive Era regulations of both business and the political parties.[35]

Reformers no doubt hoped to purify politics and bring it closer to filling the public interest by weakening party control and its connection with business. As ongoing complaints about the influence of money on politics attest, this round of reform did no such thing. But slowly and haltingly, the more stringent regulatory environment within which the parties operated helped change how campaigns raised money, gathered information, and assembled workers. When federal law banned contributions from corporations in 1907, fundraisers courted wealthy individuals as they always had. Sometimes they also aimed at smaller contributors. By the 1920s, party leaders borrowed techniques from World War I bond sales and charity organizations such as the Community Chest to orchestrate their own fund drives. Party leaders continued to gather information from local chieftains, but by the 1930s they also supplemented such intuitions with the tables and reports of statisticians and pollsters. Campaign professionals organized a workforce through attracting volunteers and, in a shortcut, membership-based interest groups and unions.[36]

Nowhere were early twentieth-century efforts to eliminate the privileged place of political parties and their "corrupt" ties to business as thorough as in the West. A quick tour of California politics can clarify the consequences of reform. Campaign managers adapted to the regulations that hobbled political parties that, together with technological developments, changed the business of campaigns.

Between 1893 and 1911, Californians, furious at the "ownership" of their government by the Southern Pacific railroad, struck out at party rule. They instituted some of the standard reforms—the initiative, referendum, and recall—designed to return government to the people. California progressives went further in curbing the power of the apparently corporate-controlled political parties. A strict civil service regime would remove nearly all state patronage at the disposal of the parties. The 1893 Purity in Elections law required candidates to create oversight committees that tracked the money they raised and spent and limited their spending to the salary of the office. In 1915, voters rejected through a referendum statewide ballots that would erase references to political parties. But California adopted a cross-filing system that allowed candidates to run under any or all party labels in primaries, and forbade the parties from endorsing candidates in primary elections.

As sociologist Elizabeth Clemens observes, California "[r]eformers dealt near fatal blows to the parties, which were saved by the continuing relevance of partisanship for federal elections." Still, candidates had to raise money, find workers, gather information, and communicate with voters. Their ties to interest groups became important, as various citizen's organizations could supply labor, policy expertise, and some campaign funds. One beer and liquor industry lobbyist, the legendary Artie Samish, became an unofficial boss from 1930s and 1940s, providing money and advertising to candidates who pledge to back his concerns. Republicans, and somewhat later the Democrats, formed clubs that launched the careers of candidates and provided connections to state party networks. The most enduring response to the problem of running campaigns with feeble parties brought together interest groups, campaign funds, and loose party organizations: political consultants who specialized in bringing order out of chaos.[37]

Campaigns, Inc., was the first, most famous, and successful of these. Founded by Clem Whitaker, a former newspaper reporter and lobbyist, and Leone Baxter, a reporter who later married Whitaker, the firm took shape in 1933 out of work on a ballot question concerning a Central Valley water project. In addition to supplying small-town California newspapers with (carefully nonpartisan) editorials and features through their California Feature Service, Campaigns, Inc., racked up an impressive series of victories for their clients on ballot questions, including the defeat of the "Ham and Eggs" pension plan in 1939. The firm also provided corporate public relations, often conducted through articles and editorials published through the Feature Service. Or, as Clem Whitaker Jr. explained in a letter to the head of the National Cotton Council of America, interested in the uses of cottonseed oil, "Our firm's specialty is conducting public education campaign ads, in California, through our California Feature Service, we are ideally equipped to do a thorough job on a given subject of such intense potential interest to the State as that of imitation ice cream."[38]

Campaigns, Inc., might try to change the image of cottonseed oil, but it offered fuller services on policy and political questions. While their work on ballot questions spanned a variety of interests, their candidates clustered in the center of the Republican party. Their clients, who included Earl Warren, Goodwin Knight, and Dwight Eisenhower's California campaign, supported "individual initiative and personal responsibility; the free operations of our economic society; reasonable freedom from government control and directive," in Baxter's words. Taking an advertising firm's traditional 15 percent cut, Whitaker, Baxter, and a small staff coordinated all aspects of a campaign, from fund-raising to advertising to what clubs and party chairmen ought to be doing or saying for their candidate.[39]

The 1954 campaign for Goodwin Knight for governor had the hallmarks of a Campaigns, Inc., effort. Whitaker and Baxter aimed, as they had with Earl Warren, to carry a plurality in both the Democratic and Republican primaries. This made for an expensive primary campaign, but if successful, it saved money: by focusing attention on the relatively smaller proportion of voters who turned out in the June election, there might be no credible opposition in November. In consultation with Knight and the United Republican Finance Committee, Campaigns, Inc., turned to early fund-raising. The primary budget of $600,000 seemed high to some activists. But even if they failed to make the general election superfluous, a big primary win would demonstrate nationally that Republicans could win California without "compromising their principles or embracing New Dealism."[40]

One Whitaker/Baxter advantage was their ability to advance substantial funds to a campaign, which eliminated the need for a campaign to live from contribution check to contribution check. Both collections and expenditures were centralized in the firm's San Francisco office. Meanwhile, they coordinated fund-raising efforts. There were separate northern and southern California divisions. There were divisions representing a great many industries—insurance, banking, medical, dental, canning, law, funeral, newspapers, construction, dry cleaners, real estate, dairy, and film among them. There were groups: Hungarian, Chinese, Armenian, Mexican, Jewish, Italian, French, and Swiss; women and African Americans; labor and farm organizations and rubbish collectors; the National Association for the Advancement of Colored People, the Knights of Columbus, assorted civic associations, and women's organizations; and skiers and bowlers. In each case, a person with wide contacts who supported Knight would send out letters (which Campaigns, Inc., had provided) to their circle or organize fund-raising events. Regular party activists also searched for contributions among their regular contacts. There were problems—trying to make sure that major donors were not contacted too often, fund-raisers who promised too much in return for support, fund-raisers who simply failed to produce. But the system kept contributions coming in, which were followed by letters of thanks from Knight and campaign pins.[41]

Campaigns, Inc., followed the same pattern in organizing campaign workers. To save money, the campaign did not send out mass mailings; instead, volunteers were to get Knight materials in the hands of voters in a door-to-door effort. There were Democratic committees charged with finding Democratic support for Knight in the primary. When the head of the first did not seem to be working, one of Whitaker and Baxter's contacts identified Irene Dockweiler, "who has more savvy about campaigning than almost any other woman I know in Southern California," to replace him. Regional and county committees received literature to distribute and records of Knight's speeches to listen to at rallies. Women's organizations received material, as their members might have the time to get it in the right hands. A few individuals, such as an African-American Baptist minister, received support and literature to hand out.[42]

Campaigns, Inc., tightly prescribed what and when workers said and did. The firm had designed a campaign plan with a theme and rhythm, and they did not trust party workers to improvise. A campaign plan sent to chairmen of Knight-for-Governor committees detailed what Knight believed, what the issues were, what campaign materials would be forthcoming and how they should be used, and what their organizations should be doing. An internal memo congratulated Baxter on her work: "I groaned inwardly at seeing some of the techniques so beautifully spelled out," the staffer wrote, adding that it "will be a real lifeline." Whitaker and Baxter did not trust enthusiasm. "We've found through the years that Local and County Campaign Headquarters manned by Volunteers haven't much of a notion as to how many pieces of literature they can distribute effectively," they wrote to the Southern California chairman. "As a matter of fact, it's hard for them to see much difference between 5,000 and 50,000 pamphlets. We always invite them to request literature—but we try to anticipate their needs and figure out ahead what amounts of literature they can distribute effectively and without waste in each area." When the campaign continued into the fall, "Field Men" visited county organizations to let them know what they needed to do to close the deal.[43]

By the Whitaker-Baxter method, campaigns had pace. Volunteers and workers had to be kept interested—a love for politics or Knight's cause, not patronage, motivated them. But voters were not likely to pay attention to the election until the day was close. Therefore Campaigns, Inc., held back spending until near the end—typically 75 percent in the last three weeks. And they planned where the spending would go well in advance. Whitaker and Baxter explained in January that they aimed for "the real publicity blasts about six weeks before election day." For that they prepared a "backlog of strong and newsworthy statements to be hung on leaders in every area, faction, profession, and group of every nature" and advised having the "Organization Department working on lining up such leaders, who will be willing and eager to be quoted when the time comes."[44]

Knight did not win both primaries, but he did carry the state in November. Campaigns, Inc., furthered its reputation as a newfangled kind of machine politics in Carey McWilliams's depiction. Whitaker and Baxter were hardly bosses in the traditional sense—they built no machine and had little patronage, and that through their wide contacts among businessmen and politicians. They did, however, insist on iron rule in running campaigns, and in the process produced the sort of politics that commentators today decry: packaged, scripted, and expensive (another $250,000 went to the general election, and this before the heavy use of television). They assumed that voters paid light attention to politics; it required a consistent, easy message to penetrate them. It was a campaign run by experts. Poll-

ing firms provided information and media professionals crafted the
appeals. Party workers, in this model, were, like volunteers (and radio, television, and bumper stickers), a means of delivering the message. They were unskilled labor that needed direct guidance and had
little room to make their own decisions, much less make demands
on the state campaign.[45]

Consultants pulled together the purposely fragmented pieces of
California politics. In a state where the regulatory environment weakened the parties' ability to connect voters to government in an ac-
countable fashion, with a mobile population, and where the expanse
of its citizens' interests made organization expensive, some mechanism for coordination was necessary. As similar conditions increasingly described much of the rest of the country, technical
expertise—and the consultants who provided it—occupied a larger
part of campaigns. These "hired guns" also came to play the villain's
part in the tale of the degradation of American politics. The era of
patronage and assessments can seem almost bucolic if one believes
that campaign professionals like Whitaker and Baxter contributed
to all that ails American politics—alienated voters, plastic candidates, slick appeals, and debate about trivia.[46]

Legislation that would cut at the role of consultants, like that which
limited the political activities of public employees, is hard to imag-
ine. Instead, the preferred fix has been to go after their apparently
lifeblood—money. Campaigns have grown more expensive since the
mid-1950s. Television has been part of that, but technology alone
does not drive campaigns. There is more to both potato chip sales
and political campaigns than television ads. Campaigns require a
workforce. Over the past fifty years it has included both skilled professionals and unskilled laborers. The former can be drawn from the
parties, if they have the funds to maintain the expertise, or they can
be hired from scratch for individual campaigns. The civic minded,
who existed in 1868, 1954, and today, can supply some of the unskilled labor. But to find enough labor, incentives beyond good citi-
zenship help. Some workers hope for future political careers or to
advance their beliefs. To find ready-made groups of believers, campaigns and parties have turned to membership-based interest groups,
from the Christian Coalition to labor unions. Their members are
interested in policy, but reliance on such groups tends to draw the
parties closer to the ideological bases—and to a partisan rigidity that
many Americans also say they dislike.[47]

Campaign finance reform has wider consequences than, say, efforts to regulate potato chip ads. Over the years of debate over a variety of plans, we know some pitfalls to avoid—plans that provide incumbents even more advantages, plans that violate First Amendment rights, and plans that give one party an advantage over the other. To these considerations I would add plans that do not consider the industry as a whole. Campaigns have capital requirements, but they also need labor, internal information, and communication. Approaching campaign finance from the side of capital alone, as if money were the only thing that matters in politics, will likely produce campaigns that are even narrower and more dependent on the media and interest groups than current ones that many Americans find arid and barren.

University of Pittsburgh

Notes

1. Bradley A. Smith, *Unfree Speech: The Folly of Campaign Finance Reform* (Princeton, 1991), 42. A handy compilation and discussion of national campaign laws is Corrado, Mann, Ortiz, Potter, and Soraf, eds., *Campaign Finance Reform: A Sourcebook* (Washington, D.C., 1997).

2. I take some inspiration from the "new institutionalist" work on political economy. I have in mind, for example, John H. Aldrich, *Why Parties? The Origin and Transformation of Political Parties in America* (Chicago, 1995); Terry M. Moe, "The Politics of Bureaucratic Structure," in John E. Chubb and Paul E. Peterson, *Can the Government Govern?* (Washington, D.C., 1989); and Barry R. Weingast and William Marshall, "The Industrial Organization of Congress," *Journal of Political Economy* 96 (February 1988): 132–63.

3. The focus on Republicans here is accidental, for these campaigns records are especially good, which is not often the case with campaign finance. In 1868, the coordination of a national campaign no doubt helped with record-keeping. The Whitaker-Baxter collection at the California State Archive provides an early consultant's view of running modern campaigns, and Whitaker-Baxter handled Republican accounts as well as campaigns on ballot questions. Republicans would tend toward greater centralization than Democrats until perhaps the 1970s.

4. But on electioneering, see Robert J. Dinkin, *Campaigning in America: A History of Electoral Practices* (Westport, Conn., 1989); and Michael E. McGerr, *The Decline of Popular Politics: The American North, 1865–1928* (New York, 1986).

5. For an overview of the issues and candidates, see John Hope Franklin, "Election of 1868," in Arthur M. Schlesinger Jr., ed., *History of American Presidential Elections, 1789–1968*, vol. 3 (New York, 1985), 1247–66.

6. The most concise account of patronage, payoffs, and parties as financial organizations is Clifton K. Yearley, *The Money Machines: The Breakdown and Reform of Party Finance in the North, 1860–1920* (Albany, N.Y., 1970), especially 97–134.

7. A description of party structure is Jesse Macy, *Party Organization and Machinery* (New York, 1912).

8. On building infrastructure, see Richard H. Abbott, "The Republican Party Press in Reconstruction Georgia, 1867–1874," *Journal of Southern History* 61 (November 1995): 725–60; and Abbott, *The Republican Party and the the South, 1855–1877: The First Southern Strategy* (Chapel Hill, N.C., 1986); Eric Foner, *Reconstruction: America's Unfinished Revolution, 1863–1877* (New York, 1988), 346–79; and Lawrence M. Powell, "The Politics of Livelihood: Carpetbaggers in the Deep South," in J. Morgan Kousser and James M. McPherson, eds., *Region, Race, and Reconstruction: Essays in Honor of C. Vann Woodward* (New York, 1982), 281–348.

9. The URCC raised some funds through the sale of documents as well as through assessments; Tullock to Chandler, 26 August 1868, Chandler Papers. On the operation of the URCC, see Supreme Court of the United States, In the Matter of Newton Martin Curtis, Petition for Writ of Habeas Corpus, Brief for the Government, pp. 5–6, New-York Historical Society. Congressional Republicans formed the URCC in 1866, when it proved useful in their conflict with President Andrew Johnson. But the Union Executive Congressional Committee performed many of the same functions at least by 1864. See the undated assessment memo, Union Executive Congressional Committee; and D. N. Cooley, Secretary, Union Executive Congressional Committee, 28 October 1864, to Edwin D. Morgan, Morgan Papers, New York State Archives.

10. Untitled, 9 July 1868, and undated, "Plan for Raising Funds," Chandler Papers.

11. Untitled, 9 July 1868, Chandler Papers; and Abbott, *Republican Party in the South*, 201.

12. Chandler's career is traced in Leon Burr Richardson, *William E. Chandler, Republican* (New York, 1940).

13. Undated circular received 6 June 1868, Chandler Papers. The attempted swindle caused some confusion down the line, John Churchill to Chandler, 29 July 1868, Chandler Papers. On Maine, see, for example, James G. Blaine to Claflin, 31 August 1868; Blaine to Chandler, 10 September 1868; polling results from Maine towns, 25 August 1868; and Claflin to Chandler, 31 August 1868, Chandler Papers; Richardson, *Chandler*, 109.

14. On speakers, see A. H. Conner to Chandler, 6 August 1868. Conner to Chandler, 29 August 1868; and Union Republican State Central Committee, Indiana, to Claflin, 1 September 1868. Conrad Baker to Horace Greeley, 1 September 1868, claimed $25,000 from Louisville; a newspaper doubled the sum, *Indianpolis Jounral*, 16 and 23 September, 1868; and *New York Times*, 11 September 1868 and elsewhere. Schuyler Colfax claimed the police effort worked, Colfax to Chandler, 6 October 1868. Also see Richardson, *Chandler*, 111–13.

15. One of the few fairly hopeful early appraisals about the Indiana outlook was Godlove S. Orth to Chandler, 6 August 1868; Allen to Chandler, 11 September 1868, showed skepticism toward the demands for cash. On congressional candidates, see D. W. Voyles to Chandler, 12 September 1868 (quote); Orth to Chandler, 7 September 1868; Chandler to Orth, 8 September 1868; Orth to Chandler, 13 October 1868; and J. M. Ashley to Chandler, 13 September 1868.

16. Oliver P. Morton to Republican National Executive Committee, 7 September 1868; Chandler to Orth, 10 October 1868 (quote); J. Russell Jones to Chandler, 11 September 1868; C. M. Allen to Chandler, 12 September 1868; D. W. Voyles to Chandler, 20 October 1868; Conner to Chandler, 24 December 1868.

17. For relatively optimistic early reports and the trouble in Florida, see Jack B. Scroggs, "Southern Reconstruction: A Radical View," *Journal of Southern History* 24 (November 1958): 410–15.

18. On rallies and speakers, see John H. Caldwell to Claflin, 4 July 1868 (quote); Tullock to Chandler, 30 June 1868. Also see J. H. Jenks to Chandler, 17 June 1868;

J. M. Edmunds to Chandler, 13 June 1868 and F. W. Kellog to Chandler, 1 August 1868. On newspapers, see A. C. Fisk to Chandler, 29 August 1868; and Abbott, "Republican Party Press."

19. Claflin to Chandler, 22 July 1868 (quote); Tullock to Chandler, 17 September 1868 (quote). On Georgia, J. E. Bryan to "My Dear Sir," 5 October 1868; John H. Caldwell to Claflin, 7 October 1868; Chandler Papers; Scroggs, "Southern Reconstruction"; Olive Hall Shadgett, *The Republican Party in Georgia: From Reconstruction Through 1900* (Athens, Ga., 1964), 1–20. On the pace of funding, see Tullock to Chandler, 6 October 1868; Tullock to Chandler, 9 October 1868; Charles A. Miller to Tullock, 13 October 1868; M. A. Southworth to Chandler, 21 October 1868; and Tullock to Chandler, 13 October 1868, Chandler Papers; and Abbott, *Republican Party in the South*, 196–200.

20. John M. Morris to Claflin, 14 September 1868; Foner, *Reconstruction*, 291–345; and Franklin, "Election of 1868."

21. John M. Morris to Claflin, 24 September 1868; Scroggs, "Southern Reconstruction."

22. Foster Blodgett to Chandler, 13 September 1868; Joseph E. Brown to Chandler, 8 October 1868, Chandler Papers; Franklin, "Election of 1868"; James G. Dauphine, "The Knights of the White Camelia and the Election of 1868: Louisana's White Terrorists, A Benighting Legacy," *Louisiana History* 30 (1989): 173–90; and Allen W. Trelease, *White Terror: The Ku Klux Klan Conspiracy and Southern Reconstruction* (New York, 1971).

23. Tullock to Chandler, 27 October 1868, listed the amount the URCC spent on Southern campaigns, which included some contributions from the RNC. Louisiana received another contribution, Southworth to Chandler, 5 November 1868, perhaps of $1,000. It seems likely that both Chandler's office and the regional offices also provided funds. See also Abbott, *Republican Party and the South*, 175–203.

24. Abbott, *Republican Party and the South;* Virginia, Vincent P. De Santis, "President Arthur and the Independent Movements in the South in 1882," *Journal of Southern History* 19 (August 1953): 346–73; and Jane Dailey, *Before Jim Crow: The Politics of Race in Postemancipation Virginia* (Chapel Hill, N.C., 2000).

25. A summary of the situation in Virginia that captures much of the correspondence is Fred McWane to Paul W. Corliss, 4 April 1949; on conservatives looking for a home, see among many R. A. Harris to Sinclair Weeks, 20 July 1950, Fred McWane Papers, University of Virginia.

26. P. M. Wagenhols to Chandler, 11 September 1868. Another Ohio congressman who would lose his race pleaded for the $1,000 he believed he had been promised and complained about a $50 state assessment, J. M. Ashley to Chandler, 13 September 1868. On the Soldiers and Sailors, see, for example, Joshua T. Owen and Charles H. T. Russel to Claflin, 12 September 1868, a request for $5,000; N. P. Chipman, 19 September 1868, to Chandler; John A. Logan to Republican National Executive Committee, 19 September 1868. On later requests from other parts of the country, see E. W. Fox (Missouri) to Chandler, 24 September 1868 (who received $2,500, Claflin to Chandler, 20 October 1868); W. C. Doane, 4 October 1868, to Chandler (Pennsylvania); George Wilkes, 7 October 1868, to Committee on Finance of the National Committee (New York); J. H. Kemble to Chandler (Pennsylvania), 20 October 1868. On transportation fund, see Tullock to Chandler, 20 October 1868; New Jersey received $4,000 (Claflin to Chandler, 24 October 1868, Chandler Papers

27. David Wood to Chandler, 24 July 1868; and Charles H. Ham to Chandler, 13 November 1868. A similar complaint from Iowa is John Runnells (Republican Union State Central Committee), 25 July 1868 to Chandler. Jones had collected $15,046, with $14,000 going to Indiana; Jones to Chandler, 15 November 1868, Chandler Papers.

28. J. R. Jones to Chandler, 26 June 1868; and 27 June 1868, Chandler Papers. Claflin to "My Dear Sir," 27 July 1868, Chandler Papers. On the pace of assessments, see Tullock to Chandler, 4 September 1868; 9 September 1868; 16 September 1868; 17 September 1868; 20 October 1868; and 26 October 1868, Chandler Papers.

29. James Kelly to Chandler, 18 September 1868; Iver Phillips to Chandler, 15 August 1868; and 25 August 1868, Chandler Papers.

81 . Daniel B. Sickles to Chandler, 31 August 1868. On other contributions, see, for example, Tom Scott to Chandler, 6 July 1868; John D. Perry to Chandler, 14 August 1868; Tullock to Claflin, 4 September 1868; Jay Cooke to Chandler, 7 1868; E. Delafield Smith to Moses Grinnell, 19 September 1868; Grinnell to "My Dear Sir," 22 September 1868; and Grinnell to Chandler, 27 September 1868. Manufacturing money might well have been more important in the states, such as Pennsylvania.

31. Chandler to "My Dear General," 15 October 1868, Ulysses S. Grant Papers, Series 10, Library of Congress. Chandler moved in the opposite direction, becoming a lobbyist for various industrial and railroad concerns in the off season; Richardson, *Chandler*. On Grinnell, see Ari Hoogenboom, *Outlawing the Spoils: A History of the Civil Service Reform Movement, 1865–1883* (Urbana, Ill., 1968), 75, 90.

32. Chandler to Washburne, 19 July 1872, Elihu Washburne Papers, Library of Congress; Chandler Papers, vols. 21–34; and "Receipts and Expenditures of William E. Chandler," Ocober 1872, Edwin D. Morgan Papers.

33. Hoogenboom, *Outlawing the Spoils*.

34. On the persistence of government workers as a source of intelligence and, at times, funds, see, for example, Dorthy Ganfield Fowler, *The Cabinet Politician: The Postmasters General, 1829–1909*, rpt. ed. (New York, 1943, 1967), 246–303; through the correspondence covering 1908 through 1912 in The Papers of the Republican Campaign, Library of Congress; and Commission of Inquiry on Public Service Personnel, *Minutes of Evidence taken before the Commission of Inquiry on Public Service Personnel at Hearings held in Washington, New York, Chicago, Minneapolis, St. Paul; Seattle, San Francisco, Berkeley, Palo Alto, Los Angeles, Richmond, 1934* (New York, 1935), 65–203.

35. Richard L. McCormick, "The Discovery That Business Corrupts Politics"; Edward Chase Kirkland, *Dream and Thought in the Business Community, 1860–1900* (Chicago, 1956), 115–43.

36. Louise Overarcker, *Money in Elections* (New York, 1932); Emil Hurja Papers, Franklin D. Roosevelt Library.

37. Elizabeth Clemens, *The People's Lobby*; Arthur H. Samish and Bob Thomas, *The Secret Boss of California: The Life and High Times of Art Samish* (New York, 1971).

38. Stanley Kelley Jr., *Professional Public Relations and Political Power* (Baltimore, 1956), 39–66; Carey McWilliams, "Government by Whitaker and Baxter," *The Nation* (14 and 21 April and May 1951); and Clem Whitaker Jr. to Albert R. Russell, 10 March 1953.

39. Baxter quoted in Kelley Jr., *Professional Public Relations*, 44.

40. Whitaker and Baxter to Howard Ahmanson, 23 February 1954. A 1952 state law made winning both primaries more difficult, since primary ballots of all parties would identify candidates with party labels. Richard B. Harvey, *The Dynamics of California Government and Politics* (Belmont, Calif., 1970), 14–15; Robert J. Pitchell, "The Electoral System and Voting Behavior: The Case of California's Cross-Filing," *Western Political Quarterly* 12 (June 1959): 459–84; Dean E. McHenry, "Invitation to the Masquerade," reprinted in David Farrelly and Ivan Hinderaker, *The Politics of California: A Book of Readings* (New York, 1951), 75–81.

41. Kelley Jr., *Professional Public Relations*, 47; Whitaker and Baxter to Dr. Lewis Alesen, 23 Febrary 1954; Whitaker and Baxter to Doctor John Cline, 23 February 1954; Whitaker and Baxter to Ahmanson, 23 February 1954; Ahmanson to Goodwin Knight, 17 March 1954 (among others in this group); transcript of telephone conversation, with Mr. Robert Ledger, 3 March 1954, labeled State Rubbish Collectors Association; Nathan L. Fairbairn to Thomas Gregory, undated, deposited 15 September 1954; and untitled, 7 March 1954, list of Southern California groups, Whitaker-Baxter Papers, Box 24.

42. Zel Conn to Ahmanson, 5 May 1954; and Baxter to Russell W. Lockwood, 28 April 1954, Whitaker-Baxter Papers, Box 24.

43. Jim Dorais to Leone, undated, WB, Box 22; Plan of Campaign, undated, Box 23; Leone and Clem to Russell W. Lockwood, 20 April 1954; Whitaker and Baxter to "Fellow Campaigner," 20 August 1954, Whitaker and Baxter Papers.

44. Whitaker and Baxter to Russell Lockwood, 16 January 1954, Whitaker-Baxter Papers.

45. "McWilliams, "Government by Whitaker and Baxter."

46. Larry J. Sabato, *The Rise of Political Consultants: New Ways of Winning Elections* (New York, 1981).

47. E. J. Dionne, *Why Americans Hate Politics* (New York, 1991).

ROBERT E. MUTCH

The First Federal Campaign Finance Bills

Early in 1839, a congressional investigation into campaign fund-raising at the U.S. customhouse in New York first brought to public attention a problem in democracy that we still are trying to solve: Who should pay for our politics? By 1839, the deferential political system of the colonial era, in which government was the almost exclusive province of the old mercantile and landed elites, was well on its way out, at least in the North. Under that system, the upper classes provided the great majority of candidates for elective office and candidates paid their own campaign expenses. The transition to a more democratic system—of broader suffrage, organized parties, and professional politicians who did not have personal or family wealth—required a new way of financing campaigns. As politicians were no longer people who had money, they had to raise money.

One of those new ways was revealed by the House investigating committee. Shortly after Andrew Jackson became president, the Democratic party, or at least his faction of that new organization, began raising money from U.S. government employees by assessing them a small percentage of their salaries. This was the beginning of what became perhaps the largest source of campaign funds for both political parties in the nineteenth century. Political assessments were made possible by the still-evolving spoils system, which was itself an indirect way of funneling public funds into party treasuries.

Response to this new fund-raising practice will be examined here by looking at congressional debates over the first attempts to prohibit it. But assessments were not the primary concern even of the first bills to address them. Those bills were aimed instead at imposing much broader restrictions on the political activity of government employees. Calls for such restrictions were not new at all.

Attempts to curb electioneering by government employees go back to the first years of the American republic, and more than a century before that in Britain. The fear then was not of parties and spoils but of patronage used to create subservient legislatures and build unchecked executive power. Assessments on government employees may have been new, but they were first seen as an incremental expansion of some very old practices. Which is why some very old arguments were used against them. Congressional debates on the first campaign finance bills did raise some issues that look very much like those in today's reform debate—complaints of excessive government power, warnings about business and foreign money in elections, and appeals to the First Amendment—but in other ways they would not have been out of place in seventeenth-century England.

"Regular taxation . . . for the support of party elections"

Before 1839. Although political assessments did not become public knowledge until the House investigating committee released its report on the New York customhouse, they were well known to political insiders. Senator Daniel Webster delivered one of the first attacks on the practice in 1834, going out of his way to do so in a report on an appropriations bill. It is worth noting, though, that he did not charge that government employees actually were being assessed. What he said was that if government officers were contributing "by regular and proportionate rate . . . to objects of a party character . . . nothing can be [a] greater abuse of official station." Webster's caution on this point suggests that the practice still was so new, or so well concealed, that he had no evidence to back up an accusation.[1]

John Barton Derby showed no such caution in his 1835 account of his experiences as a deputy surveyor of the customs. He claimed that in the summer of 1830, he and other officers at the Boston customhouse were assessed about 5 percent of their salaries. The purpose of the assessment was to help repay debts incurred by the editor of the Jacksonian newspaper, the *Boston Statesman*, for its efforts in the 1828 presidential campaign. This apparently was the first time "the Tax"—Derby's term—had been imposed in Boston, and by his account it was not well received.

The idea was first mentioned at a meeting of government officers in Boston. Because those officers "obtained their offices through the distinguished exertions of the Statesman and the party which sustained it," it was "incumbent" on them to "club together, and annually, by an assessment" help retire the debt. Unfortunately for the party leaders, a motion was made and accepted to form a committee to inquire more closely into the actual amount of the debt and for what purposes it had been contracted. After this poor reception, subsequent meetings to work out the details of the assessment were held in private.

The amount of the assessments was announced a few weeks later. Derby reported that most officers paid their assessments, and those who refused to pay were told that "they would lose their offices by their pertinacity." But only five months after the payments began, all the money was refunded, reportedly "in consequence of intimations from Washington." At the same time, though, it was suggested that the officers could give their money as subscriptions to a party magazine. According to Derby, many of the officers did just that. Derby also recounts a conversation with a party leader that suggests such subscriptions had become an accepted practice. He said that the collector in Wicasset, Maine, "made all his officers pony up in supporting the Jackson paper there, and why not do the same in Boston?"[2]

It was not just customhouses. In 1838, Irvine Callender, the U.S. commissary general in Philadelphia, refused to assess the people in his office despite two requests from a Democratic committee of finance. Callender thought that citizens should be allowed to "exercise the rights of suffrage . . . without the aid of funds from public officers or institutions to give influence to any sect or party."[3]

The Customhouse Investigation. The immediate cause of the 1839 customhouse investigation was the discovery that Samuel Swartout, the collector of the Port of New York, had appropriated more than one million dollars in federal funds and lost much of it in land and railway speculation. The investigating committee eventually appointed by the House of Representatives, though, was not interested solely in Swartout's penchant for gambling with the public's money.

Whig opponents of the Van Buren administration saw the investigation as an opportunity to expose the Democrats' new practice of raising campaign finds through political assessments on employees at the New York customhouse. Assessments, however, had nothing to do with the "defalcations" of Swartout and other officers and so were not within the committee's jurisdiction. That problem was overcome when the House, which was almost evenly divided between supporters and opponents of the administration, chose committee members by ballot, electing administration critics for five of the nine seats on the investigating committee.[4]

The report eventually issued by the committee lists only two witnesses who testified that they had paid political assessments: Arent S. De Peyster, a weigher, and David S. Lyon, a deputy collector of the customs. Both men had been dismissed from their jobs by the time the committee heard their testimony. Two witnesses who were asked about their role in levying these assessments—Abraham B. Vanderpoel, a customs appraiser, and John Becker, a "collector of funds" for the Democratic party, but not a customhouse employee— refused to answer most of the questions put to them.

De Peyster testified that in the five years he held office in the customhouse he was occasionally called on to pay a "tax" of $15, but that it was only in the last two years that he had begun to pay it. "[W]hen I declined," he said, "Mr. Vanderpoel . . . observed that I ought to consider whether my $1,500 per annum was not worth pay- ing fifteen dollars for. Under the impression that it was the price of my position, I paid it." Asked if he knew why the money was being collected, he replied that it was "to support the election of persons attached to the present [Van Buren] administration." He also said that he had seen many other weighers pay the $15 assessment (HCI, 462).[5]

Lyon told the committee that he, too, had frequently been called upon to "contribute to political objects," and said that the assess- ment "was *pro rata*, according to salary," varying from one to six percent. He testified that nearly all the officers and clerks at the customhouse were assessed by "the general committee of Tammany Hall," which kept a book that listed the names of the persons as- sessed and the amount they were required to pay. Those who did not pay were warned that they would be reported to the committee. According to Lyon, almost all the officers generally paid what they were assessed (ibid., 511–12).

The only Democratic committee member who was present for De Peyster's testimony objected to the question about assessments, but was outvoted 5–1. Two Democratic members were present for Lyons's testimony, and their attempt to block the same question was voted down 5–2. The Democrats' objection was that these questions were "inquiries, not as to defalcations, but the disposition by officers of the Government of their own money," and so were about private, not public, matters (ibid., 276).

The Democrats' approach worked better with the other two witnesses. When Vanderpoel—whom De Peyster had identified as the one who collected his assessment—began to answer the majority's question about assessments of political contributions at the custom-house, one of the Democrats interrupted to tell him that "he was not bound to answer any interrogatory relating to his private affairs" (ibid., 464). Vanderpoel then refused to answer and was dismissed. The minority members then tried and failed to pass a resolution that the committee chairman inform witnesses that they were not obliged to answer any questions about their private affairs.

Becker's time on the witness stand was the most contentious. Of the thirty questions put to him about party fund-raising at the customhouse, minority members objected to five and he refused to answer seven. When he refused to answer the first questions on assessments, on the ground that the collections he made "were strictly confidential," Virginia Representative Henry Wise peppered him with questions apparently intended to uncover collusion between the witness and the minority members of the committee (ibid., 515–16). He did say that several customhouse officers had been members of "the finance committee of the general democratic republican committee," but that most had been elected to that position before being appointed to the customhouse (ibid., 518).

In their report, the committee majority did not claim that political assessments had anything to do with Swartout's misuse of funds. The question of how far assessments "may have entered into the defalcations of the late collector," the majority said, "is left to the judgment of the House." But they reached their own judgment about the broader effects of "regular taxation of public officers . . . for the support of party elections": They concluded that the practice had a "direct tendency to reduce public office to the degraded character of merchandise to be bought and sold to subordinates by a regulated annual stipend" (ibid., 249).

In the minority report, the three administration supporters claimed to see a different threat to the republic. In their mind, the committee majority made a mockery of the doctrine of states' rights by their decision that "a committee of this House . . . is authorized to go into the investigation of the private affairs of officers of the General Government in relation to their actings and doings as citizens" of their states. They jumped from this subject to that of "money spent for party purposes" and concluded that "the practice is not confined to one party, but pervades all parties in New York." They did not mention assessments directly, but did assert that "the payment was not compulsory, but voluntary." Their evidence for this statement was that De Peyster testified that "for three years out of five . . . he contributed nothing" (ibid., 278–79).

Bills to Prohibit Assessments

Representative John Bell of Tennessee introduced the first bill to prohibit assessments in January 1837, two years before the House began investigating fund-raising at the New York customhouse. Entitled "a bill to secure the freedom of elections," its first section provided that no federal government officer "shall, by the contribution of money or other valuable thing . . . intermeddle with the election of" state or federal officials.[6] As the title of his bill suggests, Bell saw political assessments as part of a larger problem.

That problem was described in the bill's preamble, which referred to two complaints about federal government officers: that they had been dismissed from office "upon political grounds, or for opinion's sake," and that they were "in the habit of intermeddling in elections . . . otherwise than by giving their votes." Both practices, Bell claimed, were clear violations of the freedom of elections. To address these problems, the bill did not stop at prohibiting federal government officers from making campaign contributions. The bill's second section provided that no one be appointed to government office "upon any agreement that such person or persons . . . shall exert his or their influence in any election."[7]

As the first attempt to prohibit a source of campaign funds, Bell's bill can be seen as the first federal campaign finance bill. But it was so only because it also was an attack on what already was called the spoils system. Supporters of the administration that had begun that system did not, however, feel inclined to defend assessments. There was no need to do that against Bell's first bills, which did not even come to a vote.[8] But Jacksonians passed up the opportunity to defend assessments even in 1840, when Bell's bill, introduced for the third and last time, did reach the floor.

"Is there, or can there be, any just exception to this proposition?" Bell asked about his proposal to ban assessments. "Is it fit that any portion of the salaries paid to the public officers, out of the common treasure, shall be given to corrupt the ballot-box and to carry elections in favor of a party?" The fact that some administration supporters were "hardy enough to deny that such a practice prevails" suggested to Bell "a prevailing sense, among many, of the enormity of such a practice."[9] No one denied the existence of assessments during floor debate, but neither did anyone defend them.

The only other opportunity for a debate on assessments came in 1839, when Kentucky Senator John J. Crittenden introduced a similar bill in the Senate. While the House investigating committee was still interviewing customhouse employees in New York City, Crittenden proposed that every government employee be prohibited from "intermeddling" in state or federal elections "otherwise than by giving his own vote."[10] The blanket ban on any participation in elections other than voting implicitly covered assessments, but these were not explicitly mentioned in the original bill.

In the Senate, too, assessments took up a very small part of the debate. Only South Carolina Senator W. C. Preston mentioned them, asking if any senator would "rise in his place and say, on his honor, that he believes Federal officers do not pay a tax, *pro rata*, for election purposes? Will any gentleman even say that he doubts it? I do not yet assert it, but do we not know it?"[11] The subject was raised once more, in an amendment proposed to save the bill. New York Senator Nathaniel P. Tallmadge proposed to apply the bill's penalties—a $500 fine and permanent disqualification for federal government office—only to the officeholders who "shall subscribe sums of money to carry on elections." The amendment was defeated 26–15.[12]

Tallmadge offered his amendment to meet the most consistent criticism of the Bell and Crittenden bills: that they violated the First Amendment. Michigan Representative Isaac E. Crary was the first to make this charge, saying that Bell's bill "looks too much like the old sedition law. It is a bill to circumscribe freedom of speech and action. . . . it violates the constitution."[13] The Senate Judiciary Committee made the same criticism in its report on the Crittenden bill, and Pennsylvania Senator James Buchanan was equally forceful on the Senate floor: "This bill is a gag law. . . . The Constitution, in language so plain as to leave no room for misconstruction, declares that, 'Congress shall make no law abridging the freedom of speech.'"[63]

South Carolina Senator John C. Calhoun agreed about the denial of rights if not necessarily about the applicability of the First Amendment. Calhoun was at best a lukewarm supporter of Van Buren's administration, and said that he approved of the bill's purpose. He nonetheless opposed it because it made no distinction "between the official and private acts of the officer as a citizen." But, he claimed, an officer's "private rights as a citizen . . . are . . . under the exclusive control of the States," over which the federal government had no authority. The proper way to solve the problem addressed by Crittenden's bill, Calhoun concluded, was "to turn back the Government to where it was when it commenced its operation in 1789."[15]

Crittenden himself appears to have been swayed a bit by these criticisms. The amendment he offered, though, would have reduced only the penalties, not the scope of prohibited activities. His amendment was rejected 25–18. Virginia Senator William Cabell Rives, like Bell, a disaffected Jacksonian, also seems to have had doubts about the bill's constitutionality despite his strong support for Crittenden's goal. Rives moved to recommit the bill to the Judiciary Committee with instructions to amend it according to resolutions he offered that would do little more than express the Senate's view that it was "improper for officers depending on the Executive of the Union to attempt to control or influence the free exercise of the elective right." This move also failed, 25–13.[16] According to the *Globe,* the Crittenden and Tallmadge amendments and the Rives motion "were voted against by all those members of the Senate claiming to be thorough friends of the Administration."[17] When the original bill came a vote, it fared even worse: it was rejected 28–5.[18]

Representative Bell, at least, cannot have been surprised by this criticism, as he had invited even worse. In 1836, in the course of attacking an appropriations bill for rivers and harbors, he decried executive interference in elections and asked if any government employees "are any longer to be safely trusted with the right of suffrage." Suggesting that "this country should take a lesson upon this subject from the practice of a Government in form less free than our own," he read from a 1782 British statute that deprived many British government employees of the right to vote.[19]

No one else took such an extreme position, and Bell himself made no further arguments in this vein once he had introduced his bill. But arguments in favor of the Bell and Crittenden bills, and even the language of the bills themselves, derived in part from the political practice and theory of seventeenth- and eighteenth-century England.

Patronage, Parties, and Campaign Funds

In the preamble to the English Bill of Rights, Parliament accused the deposed King James II of having attempted "to subvert and extirpate . . . the laws and liberties of this kingdom" by, among other actions, "violating the freedom of election of members to serve in Parliament." Among the charges against James II were that he had tried to create a compliant Parliament both by giving patronage appointments to sitting members and by having Crown officers directly interfere in parliamentary elections. In the years following the Glorious Revolution of 1688, Parliament imposed several restrictions on the participation of executive officers in elections.

Patronage and the Freedom of Elections. The fear of executive interference in elections persisted into the first years of the American republic, and were given new life by the debates over the Constitution. In 1791, Georgia Representative James Jackson proposed amending an excise bill "to prevent Inspectors, or any officers under them, from interfering, either directly or indirectly, in elections, further than by giving their own votes." He did not claim that any such interference had yet taken place, but did say that "the experience of Great Britain showed the propriety of the prohibition," and cited one of the British laws later mentioned by Bell and Crittenden. His own amendment was aimed at preventing future abuses, in particular "the dangerous influence that some future Presidents would acquire, by virtue of the power which he will possess of removing these officers."[69]

One of the first criticisms of this amendment was that it was "unconstitutional, as it will deprive them [excise officers] of speaking and writing their minds; a right of which no law can divest them." This comment by Delaware Representative John Vining was seconded by Massachusetts Representative Fisher Ames, who charged that the amendment "will muzzle the mouths of freemen" and was "repugnant to the Constitution." The one member who was not afraid to confront these criticisms directly was Maryland Representative Michael Jenifer Stone. Stone agreed that it was "painful" that "a number of citizens should be . . . deprived of their reason and speech, but . . . we must either deprive the excise officers of this privilege of interfering or give up the freedom of elections." Jackson's amendment was voted down 37–21.[21]

The term "campaign finance" would have been even more puzzling to members of Congress in George Washington's administration than to those in Martin Van Buren's. In the 1790s, the expenses incurred in seeking elective office still were paid out of a candidate's own pocket and those of his relatives and friends. But members of Congress also knew from their experience in colonial politics that executive payrolls could be an indirect source of campaign funds. Washington himself took advantage of this source in his first stand for elective office.

Washington was a candidate for the Virginia House of Burgesses from Frederick County in 1758, while on active military duty during the French and Indian War. One of the most active workers on his behalf of his candidacy was an officer under his command, a lieutenant who commanded a fort near the Frederick County seat. Not incidentally, Washington employed this same officer as the overseer of one of his Frederick County plantations.[22] There is no indication that any of Washington's contemporaries regarded this arrangement as corrupt, as an abuse of office, or even as being worthy of notice. As the colony's ruling class, the planter gentry may well have regarded government as their collective tool and hence their collective property. They also already had considerable influence over appointments made by royal governors and so did not feel unduly threatened by executive power.

The newly created office of president of the United States, though, was a different matter. None of the local elites who had been accustomed to prominence in colonial government had any reason to believe that the new executive would be easy to control. Their near-unanimous support for George Washington as the first president eased the fears of those elites, at least for the moment. But Washington also was a strong supporter of the new Constitution that created his office. The vote on Representative Jackson's amendment in 1791 was evidence that support for the new government was not nearly as strong as support for the new president.

During the House debate on that amendment, Massachusetts Representative Elbridge Gerry—who had been a delegate to the Constitutional Convention but refused to sign the final document— urged the House to pass the measure at once. Once the evil takes place, he warned, "[t]he President will then have it in his power to influence the elections in such a manner as to procure a Legislature that would not consent to a law for applying a remedy."[23] Similar warnings were repeated thirty-five years and five presidents later, when the federal government and the electorate were many times larger. In 1826, the Jacksonian majority of a Senate select committee chaired by Missouri Senator Thomas Hart Benton alerted the country to the dangers of executive influence under the presidency of John Quincy Adams: "The power of patronage, unless checked by the vigorous interposition of Congress, must go on increasing until Federal influence . . . will predominate in elections."[24] Those who held office under Adams, charged Senator Buchanan two years later, are but the "enlisted soldiers" of the administration.[25] That these remarks were not a response to anything Adams actually did as president is suggested by the absence of the specific charges of interference in elections later made against the Jacksonians themselves.

In promoting his 1837 bill, Representative Bell claimed that active participation by federal officers in the 1836 presidential election was something "no gentleman would deny."[26] He added that he had noticed a change in public sentiment. In trips back to his district, people no longer asked him what the government or Congress would do about some issue. "No, sir; the inquiry is . . . what will the *President* do? what will the *Executive* do? what will *Andrew Jackson* do?" He saw this as evidence that "there had been a transition of the Government from the hands of the regularly constituted authorities to that of the President, and from being a Government of the people to being a Government of the Executive."[27]

Two years later, in the Senate, Senator Rives said in support of Crittenden's bill that executive interference in the 1838 congressional elections was "open, systematic, and undisguised." If reinforced by a politically active corps of officeholders, he warned, executive power would "be installed in a virtual supremacy over the laws and Constitution of the country." He and Senator Preston cited Tocqueville's recently translated *Democracy in America* to support their claim that executive power in the United States was stronger than "in any other constitutional system existing in the world." To drive home the lessons of the Glorious Revolution, he quoted Locke's comments about a prince or other executive magistrate who uses patronage appointments "to corrupt the representatives and gain them to his purposes," and "openly pre-engages the electors, and prescribes to their choice such whom he has, by solicitations, threats, promises, or otherwise, won to his designs." To "new model the ways of election" in this manner, Locke said, is to "cut up the Government by the roots."[28]

As the quoted passages from Locke make clear, the arguments made by Rives and his colleagues in the opposition still were shaped by old fears about executive usurpation of the legislature. In their mind, the dangers predicted by Representative Jackson in 1791 had come to pass. In supporting Bell's 1837 bill, Kentucky Representative William Jordan Graves charged that through his control over government employees, Andrew Jackson had "corrupt[ed] the source of legitimate power. . . . this government is, to every practical purpose, thoroughly revolutionized. All power is to the Executive department."[29]

But what Whigs called executive usurpation were the political links between executive and legislative branches that resulted from the normal operation of political parties. So by the end of Andrew Jackson's administration, the old arguments were mixed with new warnings

Spoils and Parties. "[W]hither hath the mad dominion of party carried us?" Rives asked when he read the Senate Judiciary Committee's report on Crittenden's bill. Rives and his colleagues were particularly offended by a passage that also was the closest thing to a defense of the spoils system to be found in any of the congressional debates on the assessments bills.

In protesting the unconstitutionality of Crittenden's bill, the committee report emphasized the value of the activities it would proscribe. By punishing "the use of persuasion or dissuasion," the committee claimed, the bill would suppress the very activities that should be encouraged in all citizens, including officeholders. "It is as well his [the citizen's] right as his duty to discuss and promulge freely the measures of any Administration, and the character and conduct of those who support or oppose it," the committee argued. "All this is innocent and praiseworthy, even if the motive is the acquisition of office, because it promotes the public good."[30]

Rives saw this report as "the exposition and defense of a political system which relies upon party organization, party discipline, and official patronage to control and govern this mighty country." Under the "licentious motto of party pillage, 'to the victors belong the spoils,'. . . partisan service is the required return for office, as office is to be the reward of partisan service," and the "public trusts of the nation" are won by "party servility."[31] To Rives and other Whigs, parties endangered liberty because their purpose was to build political links between the legislative and executive branches.

Bell claimed that Andrew Jackson had transformed "the entire corps of public officers . . . into a Grand Committee of the Union for the management of elections, of which the chairman will be the President of the United States!" In addition to their official duties, officers now were required to provide money and to take other measures to ensure the success of their candidates. So dominant had party considerations become, Bell said, that the House of Representatives itself could not even elect a clerk or a printer "but in strict reference to party ascendancy, and the possession of the spoils."[32]

Administration supporters did not respond to these attacks with an enthusiastic defense of the spoils doctrine. They had little difficulty in defending the practice of selecting one's political supporters for appointive office, but they were conspicuously restrained on the corresponding practice of making room for those supporters by removing existing officeholders. Senator Buchanan, perhaps looking forward to his own presidency, said that selecting "able, faithful, and well-tried political friends" was "the dictate of both justice and sound policy." He said it also had been "the long-established practice of both political parties," dating back to Washington's administration.[33] Michigan Senator John Norvell demonstrated the method for handling charges of dismissing a previous administration's appointees when he contrasted the outcry against the removals made by Andrew Jackson with the silence that greeted the removals made by Whig governors in New York, Rhode Island, and Connecticut. Noting that "the first days of the Whig saturnalia" in New York had "been celebrated by the proscription of some of the best public officers," Norvell pointed out that "no holy horror of removals for political cause, no contempt for the spoils of victory, have presented any obstacle to the elevation of patriotic and office-hating Whigs to the places vacated by these removals."[34]

It was not only the spoils system that went undefended. The Jacksonian firebrands also could not bring themselves to mount a defense of party that was as passionate as the opposition's attacks. Rives's fellow Virginian, Senator W. H. Roane, did say, "I am a party man and glory in being so," and he mocked those who claimed to be above party. But he also called himself "a Democrat of the school of 1798," that is, of the Virginia and Kentucky Resolutions—the same claim made by Rives. Senator Buchanan claimed to be a party man, too, even if he did not glory in it, but he too claimed that he had "at all times . . . held to the political doctrines" of the 1798 resolutions.[35]

Apart from the Senate Judiciary Committee report that so infuriated the opposition, this was the closest these Democrats could come to an open embrace of party and spoils. And even that report treated partisan activity as though it were no more than one's civic duty, abstracted from any connection to actual political organizations. When Senator Preston said that the report had maintained that it was the duty of officeholders to be active in elections, the committee chairman, New Jersey Senator Garret Wall, denied that it had said anything of the sort. Like assessments on officeholders, party activity was something opponents criticized freely but that supporters were reluctant to defend. When it came to sources of campaign funds, though, those same supporters launched attacks of their own.

Campaign Finance. The Senate Judiciary Committee could "not believe" the implicit premise of Crittenden's bill, that "the employés of the Federal Government are more corrupt or corrupting than the employés of other bodies-corporate or politic, or of individuals." The committee acknowledged that political morality may have sunk so low as to demand legislative remedy. But it was not clear whether this alarming laxity should be attributed to officeholders or to "the officers of corporations of associated wealth."[36]

This theme was repeated several times in the debates over the Crittenden and Bell bills. Democrats blamed the "money power" for losses in the 1838 congressional elections, especially those in the nation's biggest cities. Those defeats, Senator Roane said, showed "how impotent are all your public officers against the all-corrupting power and influence of *money* . . . of associated wealth—of monopolies, of banks."[37] Arguing against Bell's 1840 bill, Tennessee Representative Harvey Watterson went further, protesting against the influence brought to bear on elections by the "tremendous money power of this country, and its natural ally, the money power of England."[38]

These charges were made outside Congress, too. Smarting from the losses in New York, President Van Buren reached the same conclusion immediately after the election. "Our story is told in one word—money," he wrote in a letter to Andrew Jackson. "The Whig merchants, manufacturers and . . . banks also raised an enormous sum of money."[39] The *New York Democratic Review*, citing "heavy contributions of money, by those individuals and classes best able and willing to contribute," attributed the losses in that state to "a more lavish and corrupt use of money than has ever before been attempted to influence an election."[40]

Both sides decried "the use of money" in elections. No one was very clear about what was meant by that vague phrase, but it does suggest awareness of something new in the way campaigns were being financed. References to the "corrupt" use of money or to money "corrupting the ballot box" probably were attempts to hold on to the familiar—bribery, intimidation, and impersonation of voters were as old as elections, practices of which both parties must have been guilty—while expressing unease with what was unfamiliar. In complaining about officeholders' assessments going to Democrats and corporation contributions going to Whigs, both sides were indirectly addressing a new question: Where should the money come from?

Conclusion

As the first systematic approach to raising campaign funds from individuals, assessments on federal government employees were a solution to the new problem of financing the politics of a mass democracy. Yet not once were they portrayed this way in any of the debates over the first assessments bills. Assessments were seen instead as but one more way of doing something that politicians had been doing more and more since the first years of the Republic: foisting off on the government the costs of their campaigns for office. Nor was public money available only to those who controlled the presidency.

The frank was one of the most important government subsidies. First enacted by the Continental Congress in 1775, and renewed by the first U.S. Congress in 1789, the frank was intended to be a public service to members of Congress and their constituents. By the time of the debates on the assessments bills, the frank had become something quite different: the "galvanic current that animates the organization of both political parties."[41] As a political funding mechanism, the frank—plus government-financed printing and government-subsidized postal rates for newspapers—almost certainly was far more important than the still-new practice of assessments.[42] Floor speeches and committee reports could be printed and distributed for free to all parts of the country and to party newspapers. In 1839, Whigs in the House used these subsidies to order 25,000 copies of the committee report on the New York customhouse, and Senate Democrats used them to order 10,000 copies of the Judiciary Committee's report on the Crittenden bill.[43] Senator Rives did object to having so many copies of the Senate report "printed for distribution among the people," but his was the only complaint.[44]

In 1840, Bell added the frank to the practices his bill would prohibit. To the now familiar provision that no government officer should interfere in elections "by the contribution of money or any valuable thing," Bell added "or by the use of the franking privilege." He equated the use of the frank with the abuse of it and called it a "species of interference" in elections.[45] No one who has followed the campaign finance reform debates of our own day will be surprised to learn that many of those who voted for this bill had voted the year before to distribute the report on the New York customhouse as franked mail. As Representative F. O. J. Smith (D-Mass.) later wrote about the frank, "neither party is disposed to dispense with it. . . . almost every member of Congress, in the House especially, feels that his re-election is more or less dependent on an active exercise of it."[46]

Unlike the frank and the newspaper subsidy, which only very gradually came to be used for party purposes, assessments were created explicitly to finance party organization. Yet assessments also can be traced back, at least partly, to the self-financed, elite politics of the deferential era. For example, the Jacksonians covered some of the costs of their 1828 campaign by requiring party members themselves to contribute. Unlike the gentry politicians of an earlier era, these people were not all wealthy. Nonetheless, the Democrats raised additional money by assessing delegates to state conventions and even those who attended local and county party meetings.[47]

The transition from the gentleman candidate who paid his own campaign expenses to the professional politician who could not did not take place along a straight line in a series of well-defined steps. This transition was effected by practical politicians as they went about the day-to-day business of managing campaigns. The problem of financing a growing democracy was seen as one of political practice, not political theory. That was at least partly because, unlike such old questions as the extent of the suffrage, the proper scope of executive power, and the use of patronage, there was precious little in the way of political theory and historical example to help legislators make sense of this new problem. Which is why the theory and history used in the assessments bills debates were more about the era that was passing than the one that was taking shape.

Notes

1. Senate Committee on Finance. 23d Cong., 1st sess., 1834, S.Rpt. 435, 1.
2. John Barton Derby, *Political Reminiscences* (Boston, 1835), 93–97. The Wicasset customhouse may have been something of a pioneer in these efforts. That possibility is raised by an 1831 complaint to the U.S. House of Representatives

about the customs collector there. The complaint was that the collector had dismissed one of his inspectors for refusing to turn over to him 25 percent of his income. The complaint alleged that others had held office under that inspector on the same terms. During the debate over whether to refer the complaint to the Treasury Department, at least one member raised the possibility that the money collected from officers went into a political fund. *Register of Debates in Congress*, 22d Cong., 1st sess., 2252–59, 3103–4.

3. Irvine Callender to Committee of Finance, Philadelphia, 28 September 1838, Martin Van Buren Papers, Library of Congress.

4. A Whig paper in Philadelphia reported that the administration had "brought the whole strength of party discipline" to bear in a failed attempt to get "a packed committee of six Loco Focos and three Whigs." The committee finally chosen "consists of men a majority of whom will point out and expose . . . the rottenness of the system." *Poulson's American Daily Advertiser*, 5 February 1839, 3.

5. Quotations from the House investigating committee will be cited in the text after the abbreviation HCI, for *Report of the Committee of Investigation on the Subject of the Defalcations of Samuel Swartout and Others*, 25th Cong., 3d sess., H.Rpt. 313, 462.

6. *Congressional Globe*, 24th Cong., 2d sess., 1837, 124. Bell had been an early supporter of Andrew Jackson, but by 1837 the two men were political enemies. The break began with Bell's opposition to administration policy on the Bank of the United States. However, Jackson still considered the congressman a friend even after Bell won election as speaker of the 23rd Congress with the votes of Jackson opponents. But Bell's outspoken opposition to Jackson's choice of Martin Van Buren as the Democratic party candidate for president in 1836 caused Jackson to "read . . . Bell out of the party." (Joseph Howard Parks, *John Bell of Tennessee* [Baton Rouge, 1950], 112.) Bell later became a Whig and in 1841 was appointed secretary of war by President William Henry Harrison. In 1860, he ran for president on the Constitutional Union ticket.

7. *Congressional Globe*, 24th Cong., 2d sess., 1837, 124.

8. Bell's first bill was not even sent to a committee, perhaps because it was introduced close to the end of the 24th Congress. Bell noted that objection, but said he believed his chosen time to be "the only period when it was possible that a subject of this description could receive an impartial investigation and decision." *Congressional Globe*, 24th Cong. 2d sess., 1837, 127. The bill was referred to a select committee when Bell introduced it again a year later, but it still did not get to the floor for debate or vote. See ibid., 25th Cong., 2d sess., 1838, 190, 209, 224. The only debate on the second bill came in the form of incidental comments during the highly partisan exchange on the subject of President Van Buren's annual message for 1839. See, for example, the remarks of Michigan Representative Isaac E. Crary in ibid., 25th Cong., 3d sess., 1839, Appendix, 157.

9. Ibid., 26th Cong., 1st sess., 1840, Appendix, 832.

10. Ibid., 25th Cong., 3d sess., 1839, Appendix, 157. Crittenden made a long speech in support of his bill on 8 February, but the text is not in the *Globe* or in his personal papers.

11. Ibid., 343. It is interesting that, five years after Daniel Webster's reluctance to claim that government employees were in fact being assessed for political contributions, Senator Preston still was not ready to assert it. Preston made this speech on 13 February 1839, two weeks before the official date of the House report that published testimony about assessments.

12. Ibid., 27 February 1839, 213.

13. Ibid., Appendix, 157.

14. Ibid., 204.

15. Ibid., 234, 237. Calhoun voted for the Crittenden and Tallmadge amendments, but not for the original bill. Ibid., 27 February, 1839, 213.

16. Ibid.

17. Ibid., Appendix, 412.

18. Ibid., 27 February 1839, 213.

19. Ibid., 24th Cong., 1st sess., 1836, Appendix, 751. The statute was 22 George III, C. 41.

20. *Annals of Congress*, 1st Cong., 3d sess., 1791, 1924–25.

21. Ibid., 1925–27. Representatives Vining and Ames's references to the Constitution were not to the First Amendment, which had not yet been ratified and was not added to the Constitution until 15 December 1791. Most of those who voted for Jackson's amendment were later identified with Thomas Jefferson and the Democratic-Republicans, and most who voted against it were later identified as Federalists. However, most members who had been delegates to the Constitutional Convention, including Virginia Representative James Madison, voted against the amendment.

22. See Robert E. Mutch, "Three Centuries of Campaign Finance Law," in Jerold Lubenow, ed., *A User's Guide to Campaign Finance Reform* (Lanham, Md., 2001).

23. *Annals of Congress*, 1st Cong., 3d sess., 1791, 1927.

24. *Register of Debates in Congress*, 19th Cong., 1st sess., Appendix, 1826, 133, 136.

25. Ibid., 20th Cong., 1st sess., 1828, 1374.

26. *Congressional Globe*, 24th Cong., 2d sess., 1837, 124.

27. Ibid., 128.

28. Ibid., 25th Cong., 3d sess., Appendix, 410, 411. He quoted Tocqueville's comment that because "American functionaries" were "protected by the opinion, and backed by the cooperation, of the majority, they venture upon such manifestations of their power as astonish an European. By this means habits are formed in the heart of a free country which may some day prove fatal to its liberties." *Democracy in America*, chap. 15, "Effects of the Unlimited Power of the Majority upon the Arbitrary Authority of the American Public Officers." Senator Preston also cited this passage. The John Locke quote is from *The Second Treatise on Government*, chap. 19, ¶222.

29. Ibid., 24th Cong., 2d sess., Appendix, 317–18.

30. Ibid., 25th Cong., 3d sess., Appendix, 158–59.

31. Ibid., 407, 409, 412.

32. Ibid., 26th Cong., 1st sess., Appendix, 833, 834.

33. Ibid., 207–8.

34. Ibid., 182.

35. Ibid., 188, 191, 205, 210.

36. Ibid., 158, 160.

37. Ibid., 186.

38. Ibid., 26th Cong., 1st sess., Appendix, 370.

39. Martin Van Buren to Andrew Jackson, 16 November 1838. Martin Van Buren Papers, Library of Congress.

40. "The New York Election," *United States Democratic Review*, January 1839, 4.

41. F. O. J. Smith, "The Post-Office Department," *Hunt's Merchants Magazine*, December 1844, 530–31.

42. In the Post Office Act of 1792, Congress expanded the frank, building on colonial custom by allowing newspapers to be mailed anywhere in the postal system for a nominal fee. By 1800, observers already were commenting on how the newspaper subsidy was spreading the "rage of party." Richard R. John, *Spreading the News: The American Postal System from Franklin to Morse* (Cambridge, Mass., 1995), 40.

43. *Congressional Globe*, 25th Cong., 3d sess., 1839, 213, 151.

44. Ibid., Appendix, 407.

45. Ibid., 26th Cong., 1st sess., Appendix, 832.

46. Smith, "Post-Office Department," 530–31. In his 1835 book, Derby called Smith, a Democratic member of the U.S. House of Representatives from Massa-

chusetts, an "excrescence of party," presumably because newspapers Smith published vigorously disputed Derby's accounts of events at the Boston customhouse. (Derby, *Reminiscences*, 95.) Four years later, though, as a member of the House committee investigating the New York customhouse, Smith was silent on the matter of assessments and did not sign the minority report. An earlier contributor to *Hunt's* wanted to abolish the frank for much the same reason that Smith wanted to keep it: "The present system, let it be conducted as it may, can never, in the nature of things, be wholly free from political abuses, and is always in danger of being converted into a mere political machine." B. Bates, "Post-Office Reform—Cheap Postage," *Hunt's Merchants Magazine*, February 1840, 266.

47. Robert V. Remini, *The Election of Andrew Jackson* (Philadelphia, 1963), 80–86.

MARK WAHLGREN SUMMERS

"To Make the Wheels Revolve
We Must Have Grease":
Barrel Politics in the Gilded Age

It was a typical election year in Philadelphia. The nation's freedom lay at peril, and everything depended on thousands of day laborers, up for sale at one to five dollars apiece on election day. That, at any rate, was what one observer warned Republicans in 1868. "Whichever party is the most plentifully supplied with the 'root' will command the vote of these honest 'Bones and Sinews,' in spite of fate!" he predicted. "The democracy for once, are in funds to repletion, & they intend to 'win or die'!"[1]

As it turned out, the Democrats neither won nor died, but the impression is graven as deep in popular historians' minds as it was in that Philadelphia Republican's, that politics, in the late nineteenth century, was drowned in the slush funds of campaign finance. One image sums up the impression best: Joseph Keppler's 1889 cartoon, "Bosses of the Senate." Glowering from the galleries, towering over the puny solons riffling through their papers below, were the real powers of the day, the money-bags of corporate capitalism.[2] It is a compelling picture, and in an age when PACs and soft money dominate the headlines, almost comforting in its assurance that once there was a time that was worse, far more beholden to big money than the ones that followed. There is just one problem with it: it is only partly true.

To hear the party editors of Gilded Age America tell it, every election floated on a neap-tide of money, washing out every bulwark of fair, free democratic choice. Regularly, scare stories spread of war chests of several million dollars, and individual votes selling for thirty dollars apiece. No sum seemed too fabulous, no conspiracy too incredible, not to be tried. What could be more sensational than the "confession" of Ohio gubernatorial candidate George Hoadly, that he had spent $50,000 winning the Cincinnati primary elections? (Hoadly's "confession," it turned out, was his failure to scotch a free-floating rumor). Somehow, the other side could raise fabulous sums, just to carry a single state in a presidential year: $258,000 to carry Maine in 1884, say, or $400,000 to wean Alabama from the Democracy in 1892.[3]

Parties had any number of good reasons for overstating what the enemy spent. Voters could only be stirred up by a sense of imminent peril, and the money-bag bogeyman joined that whole line of other terrors: "British gold," "Rebel claims," Knights of the Golden Circle, and the like.[4] Putting one's opponents in the wrong, by suggesting that their cause was too unjust to win on its own merits, certainly eased the process of arguing, especially if, on the issues, one's own party had the weaker case. Figuring out the comparative advantages of specific and ad valorem duties baffled some voters and bored others. But anybody could understand the danger of cheap imports (bribe and ballot in hand) from Kentucky into Indiana just before the polls opened. The scaremongers were not just being cynical. If politicians' private letters are any guide, they gulped down unbelievable reports with gusto. A month before Indiana's 1868 election, a Republican operative in the south of the state was sure that the foe had put in $135,000 already. His "proof" came "not only in the appearance here and there of strange faces but in unaccountable change of Republicans of note and influence in almost every part of the state." Level-headed congressmen warned that the other side had "unlimited means at its finger ends," or was about to raise millions on millions.[5]

This was fairy-tale finance. Those in the know made more precise calculations of what their own side spent, and always their national committees made do on amounts that, compared to rumor, seemed trifling. One historian guessed that the Republican national committee spent about $200,000 in 1868. An itemized account from William E. Chandler of New Hampshire, a privileged insider in more than one party campaign, put it at a little over $63,000, with a few hundred dollars left over, though of course it had a partner organization in Chicago that raised $15,000 more, and other contributors were advised to help out local and congressional campaigns without going through the national organization. Expenses and collections certainly rose over time, the more so as campaign machinery became more sophisticated, but the upward limit remained surprisingly low. Years later, Chandler would claim that his party's national committee never had more than half a million dollars to use in any presidential year before 1896. Nor had their Democratic counterparts. In a presidential year, a party's central committee, even in an important state considered itself lucky to have as much as Hoadly allegedly put into a one-day city primary.[6]

Necessarily, national committees were forced to pick and choose where to expend precious resources. Pennsylvania might well be the battleground in 1868. Voting for state offices as it did a month before the presidential race ended, it, like Indiana, could serve as an unofficial poll to how well the competing parties were doing. Republicans had no doubt of it, and they were quite right: when the returns came in, the results from Indiana, Pennsylvania, and Ohio were so disheartening that leading Democrats embarked on a mad—and as it proved, abortive—scheme to dump their ticket and fashion a new one.[7] A narrow defeat in Indiana in 1880 took the heart out of Democrats in the last three weeks of the campaign, just as North Carolina's August state elections in 1872 did for their party down south. With good reason, politicians for the October states could insist on priority, when money was to be handed out, and, generally, got the lion's share.[8] But amid the talk of millions, what a tawny, scrawny lion it was! Stressing the vital importance of carrying Pennsylvania in 1868, James A. Briggs, of the state central committee, set his hopes unrealistically high. "If fifty thousand dollars could be sent here," he wrote the national Republican chairman, "it would be the best investment that could be made for the success of our party in this canvass." From various campaign committees, Indiana may have received $50,000 in all. In 1872, the loud cries of panic from Indiana and the national prominence of Senator Oliver Morton, whose reelection depended on electing a legislature that fall, spurred the committee to special pains on his behalf. Even then, the national committee's cash donations, a fortnight before the election, only amounted to some $40,000, which, the chairman commented, was treating the state "handsomely." At that point, with Pennsylvania's equally crucial election looming, the committee had spent only $7,500 there, and it applied itself to sweetening the pot lavishly over the days that followed. But even so, the numbers were in the tens of thousands, not the hundreds or millions, and perhaps no more than $75,000 in all.[9]

September states usually got less, because the two Northern ones—Maine and Vermont—were usually too reliably Republican to show much about how strong the parties' national strength would be in November. Still, Maine could always draw on the party war chests. Promising "a splendid campaign and a glorious victory," Congressman James G. Blaine reminded party managers in 1868 that "to make the wheels revolve we must have *grease.*" The Republican national chairman, William Claflin, balked at sending "that gunpowder for Maine," pleading poverty, but he was brought round by some hard persuading. Even so, the amounts were nothing like rumor had it. At a time when Democrats were describing massive slush funds— $20,000 for one congressional district alone, and that presumably just one installment on a far larger sum—the national committee was sending $5,000 for the whole state, and, in case that was not enough, furnished one of the campaign orators with $500 more to tender the state committee. When the final scores were counted up, Maine received only $15,000.[10]

If the pivotal states received comparatively modest amounts, those where victory seemed less assured, and those not voting until November, were badly slighted. It was all very well to speak of national support for the struggling Republican parties of the South. No state organizations needed help so badly; none had so few newspapers to champion their cause and magnates to bankroll their campaigns, or so many individual members too poor to contribute a penny on their own. It would have been good to carry some southern states in 1868, and the Republican party could use them as insurance against unexpected losses up north. But the Republicans could win without a single electoral vote south of the Ohio, if things worked out right, and New York's thirty-odd electoral votes mattered far more than South Carolina's half-dozen. With two weeks of the campaign left to go, Arkansas had received just $3,000, North Carolina and Georgia $5,000 apiece, and Alabama $3,000. There might be more to come, but it would be a couple thousand at most, not the tens of thousands that the parties so badly needed.[11] In the years that followed, as the odds of success diminished, so did the attention and the generosity. Louisiana may have got $5,000 in 1868, and only received $3,000 four years later—and it was one of the states Republicans had the best chance of carrying, with work.[12]

That left little or nothing for congressional candidates. In off years, when no presidential candidate was at stake, the national committee remained moribund, and its collection of funds was far more haphazard and unsuccessful. Congressmen often had to take care of themselves, and often that meant providing for the expenses personally or turning to a congressional campaign committee that doled out dribs and drabs, and then only to the worthiest applicants.[13]

All of these cautions should temper any notion of Gilded Age politics as afloat on a sea of campaign spending. Yet we would be equally wrong to underestimate the amount of money used. The fact is, campaign costs are beyond reasonable calculation. The figures that the national committees discussed were not the cost of campaigning; they were simply the national committee's share of the burden. For the very nature of the federal system assured that most of the expenses would be impossible to track down, much less add up. State and local organizations and private associations covered much of the expense in a campaign.[14] In most cases, they covered the local election-day costs, provided the volunteers and paid poll-watchers, bought the costumes, and hired the halls. Businessmen gave on their own, or issued tracts to waken the voters on certain issues that suited one party's purposes—a nineteenth-century equivalent of soft-money advertising.[15]

Indeed, a realistic cost analysis for a campaign would need to include all those services that were provided without money actually changing hands. Unlike today, it was the work of people on the public payroll, or of volunteers. A campaign parade, for example, was as much a means of building morale and an advertisement for the cause as any television spot would be a century later. Marchers carried mottoes, summing up pithily the essential points of the contest, and marking the difference between parties. A large turnout could dampen the opposition's ardor for going to the polls by convincing it that the contest was lost beyond retrieval; a poor showing on the streets, conversely, could encourage them to redouble their efforts toward victory. Yet for all this publicity, the party's expenses were considerably less because most of the labor—the manpower, the floats, the transparencies, were provided at the participants' expense. Government workers' efforts were certainly paid for, in the sense that taxpayers footed the bill for their salaries and indirectly absorbed the costs when public employees took time away from their duties to attend caucuses and round up the votes; all this, too, was unquantifiable.

Finally, the need for brochures and propaganda—the campaign of "education," as it was euphemistically called—was considerably less because the intensely partisan press did the job so much more thoroughly. Not just the editorials but the front-page stories worked to rouse the faithful and discredit the opposition. Most of these advantages were beyond calculation, but that does not mean they had no financial value. They did, a very great one.

Where did the money go? Most of it was applied to legitimate campaign costs. Used judiciously, a good manager could print five and a half million documents for thirty thousand dollars.[16] Speakers gladly devoted their time to the party, provided their expenses were taken care of, but their eloquence took on a truer ring if the managers reimbursed them for their time as well—say, one hundred dollars a week. Razzle-dazzle street theater, one essential of the Gilded Age campaign, never came cheaply. Even where most of the expenses of a campaign parade were given to clubs and local organizations or to individuals, state and local committees ended up footing much of the bill. For the Republican city committee in Boston, for example, a torchlight parade cost in the thousands, and at the campaign's end, they were still scrounging to find the $1,800 due to suppliers.[17]

Presses had to be bought or built for the cause, where none existed, and newspaper reporters squared. Newspapers were smaller and less expensive than in the twentieth century, though the costs of starting up were rising feverishly in the 1880s and 1890s, as the demand of readers increased for features beyond the partisan politics served up a generation before. A campaign paper could be started— or even a campaign humor magazine, if the opposition already was well served that way. In 1872, with the German vote apparently hanging in the balance, Republicans made the mistake of not scrounging up the money fast enough for buying the support of Cincinnati's German newspaper, and they kicked themselves liberally for months after at their folly. (The national committee, unable to pay the whole expense for the bargain and sale, had turned to the administration for help, and the necessary parties had been off on vacation or failed to see the importance of the investment.) They were forced to provide $5,500 for a ready-made new German newspaper of their own.[18]

Where no party organ existed, the state and national committees found strong reasons to set one up. With only four Republican newspapers in Kentucky, three of them weeklies, it was impossible to get the word out. Meetings could not be announced or speakers advertised if the local press establishment refused to publish them, as usually they did. Indeed, at its worst, a news blackout could ignore the existence of an opposition party completely, denying readers even awareness of the name of the candidate against whom Democrats were running. Nobody doubted that a party subsidy for the Louisville *Commercial* would give Republicans value for money. The only questions were how large a subsidy it needed and what form it would take.[19] Other papers asked for a few hundred dollars to make up for their debts, or to buy more type, or to pay for expenses, and, of course, a well-placed editor could make money by being given the local post office or being awarded the printing contract for the state or city, or the right to publish the advertisements of the federal government, usually at a price higher than competitive bidding would have provided.[20]

Ballots themselves were a very substantial expense as well. Take a typical election day in the early 1880s in New York City. The parties would have to pay to erect and man ticket booths near the polls, print their own ballots, some of which they mailed to potential voters and many of which they peddled on election day. Just addressing and posting the ballots cost each organization $12,000; typesetting and printing the Democratic city ticket employed two hundred and fifty typesetters and six hundred women who folded and bunched the ballots for partisans' use. The forty-eight million ballots printed in 1886 were a small item on a very large bill. Add in the peddlers themselves hired at five dollars for the day, and the experts' guess that all the different parties spent $250 for the mechanics of holding an election on each of the city's 608 election districts seemed quite reasonable.[21]

Beyond that, there were the many incidental expenses connected to election day. In 1888, Philadelphia's major parties bought up some one hundred thousand poll-tax receipts to enable their poorer supporters to vote and to induce other delinquents to vote right. Party organizers paid the expense for procuring naturalization papers for the foreign-born. Carriages needed to be hired, to bring the infirm to the polls, and compensation paid to workers whose wages were docked for the time they took off to cast a ballot.[22]

When insiders spoke of money needed for spending "judiciously" on an election, though, they may well have been using one of the many guarded terms for that other inevitable expense that both parties denounced and both did willingly: buying up the floating vote or buying off local leaders who might otherwise cause trouble. Kentucky and Delaware voters were notoriously venal, and in some upstate New York towns, the so-called "floaters" sat on the fence-rows near the polling place, waiting for the best bid. So common was the practice in Rhode Island that one reporter wrote up election day in stock-exchange terms. "On that day the market for votes opened at five dollars, with a brisk demand and strong upward tendency," he noted. "Many holders declined to enter the market, even to the extent of naming figures, preferring to stimulate inquiry by an affectation of confidence in the value of their franchises. . . . The highest point was reached at 3 p.m., when $10 was freely offered and accepted. The published quotations, however, by no means represent the real strength of the market. A very large number of private transactions took place," and "as much as $50 was realized for a single vote." The onlooker noted that complaints were rife about sellers who took pay from both sides and promised exclusive rights of delivery to both. "It is needless to point out that conduct of this kind is detrimental to the interests of sellers," he noted sternly, "and if continued at subsequent sales will have a tendency to diminish the value of their wares."[23]

Even dyed-in-the-wool partisans wanted a share of party money. The money did not mar their judgment at all; they would never have voted for the opposition. They were simply claiming a reward for services rendered and compensation for attendant inconveniences.[24] The assumption behind the spoils system was that those who did the work should get the benefits. Politicians who worked to organize the party would get their reward hereafter, in jobs and contracts; those they induced to show up on election day often felt that they had the right to ask for a reward immediately. How, morally, did a dollar in the hand differ from a clerk's desk in the hereafter?

Vote-buying was a delicate art because ethics varied from one floater to the next, and so did their prices, though one or two dollars was a common rate for whites most places, and twenty-five cents about as low a rate as southern blacks would accept. If the *New York Sun* was right, country prices were usually higher because the purchasers were unable to buy in bulk. There when the contest was close, an enterprising spirit might make as much as ten to twenty dollars (in hotly contested towns in New Hampshire, reformers charged, prices went four times that high in 1867, while Canadian Frenchmen were bought by the platoon for $15 apiece). Upcountry Tennessee villagers, apparently, could be bought for as little as a glass of whiskey, a plug of tobacco, or a pound of coffee, though a dollar or two was the going rate.[25]

Vote-buying added to parties' costs, and so did thwarting the rascals, the repeaters and "colonizers" from other states, the armies of strangers sheltered in city flophouses that trooped to the polls to vote under the names of the dead, absent, and inconveniently late electors still registered on the books—when any real registration procedures existed at all. When police themselves were partisan tools, and when most states had only halfhearted supervision of a general election (and none at all of a party primary), the party organization itself would have to enforce an honest result with poll-watchers. "The Democrats resort to all sorts of tricks, such as colonizing voters," a campaign speaker in Indiana warned in 1868, "and those tricks cannot be counteracted without a heavy outlay of money."[26]

So money was a must. The problem was, where and how to raise it. Democrats loved to leave the impression that the Robber Barons paid Republicans' way. True enough, corporations did give to either side, when their own financial interest seemed at stake. In every campaign, party leaders plotted to open up wallets up and down Wall Street. "If we could only get 1/10th of one per cent paid up as Insurance by the capitalists who will lose just one hundred times that if [Horace Greeley] comes in we should be too rich," railroad financier John M. Forbes remarked in 1872. The Republican national committee issued a circular to national banks in 1884, reminding their directors that Democratic victory might doom their charters, now up for renewal. One committeeman tried to have a like circular sent to the transcontinental railroads, written "to strike them in a tender spot."[27]

In fact, few companies, *as* companies, were willing to go even so far as a well-heeled individual. By and large, business firms did not produce great sums; individual officers might, and they might do so with the company's advantage in view, though more often because of their own partisan loyalties, and the way in which partisanship made them see what the company's advantage would be: it was just as easy, say, for a woollens manufacturer to argue that low-tariff Democrats were in the company's best interest because they would afford him cheaper raw material as it would be to argue that high-tariff Republicans suited the enterprise best because they would hinder foreign imports.[28] Soliciting corporate funding on behalf of either party also carried a risk. Unless one side offered an advantage too plain to gainsay, directors' partisan loyalty would come into play. Let a company fund Republicans' campaign and Democrats would protest. They might even storm into court with charges of misfeasance. Offending either side had additional risks. Incensed at the stinginess of John Murray Forbes in 1884, the Republican national committee sent its Nebraska and Iowa managers to pay the railroad executive a special visit and remind him that "if the C B & Q is going to be Democratic in the East it is not going to have Republican shelter in the West & it is mainly in the West & mostly in our two States."[29]

That corporate reluctance helps explain why the GOP had to play up the difference between parties on the tariff issue. Without unusual exertions, most businesses would be listless about modest reductions like the Mills bill in 1888. They were not about to fry their own fat as a public service, unless a free-trade scare sent *frissons* into the boardrooms. Ironmongers and steelmakers had special reasons to fear Democratic tariff-tinkers, but Quay had to bolster party appeals with a personal visit before he could extract $100,000 from them. "With all the immense interests of the Tariff at stake, I don't think a single manufacturer gave $20,000," James G. Blaine complained after the 1884 campaign. "I doubt if one gave $10,000."[30]

State races, like Ohio's, needed smaller donations, but they also were less likely to get them. "I have no doubt that there are hundreds of business men in the cities of New York and Philadelphia who would willingly give money to help us in the contest, as they certainly ought," Senator John Sherman wrote in 1885 as his own election approached. As Secretary of the Treasury, he had done them good service, as senator still more so, and while he "would not feel at liberty even to suggest the topic, from motives of delicacy," there was nothing to keep Arthur L. Conger, the Republicans' chief fundraiser in the state, from doing so. Talking $10,000 out of "the wealthy and liberal" Republicans in New York did not seem beyond Conger's powers.[31]

Conger's efforts were mixed at best. In New York, a Republican ally, attorney C. W. Moulton, reported "a growing feeling of alarm" among the party's friends about the Ohio canvass. "The apprehension is so great that I think there is a genuine desire to aid in almost any way," he assured Conger. Any way, as it turned out, except by opening their checkbooks. A week before the election, he had not been able to scrape together one cent. In Pittsburgh, a maker of cast steel declared that Republican victory was vital to his interests and those of anyone with a stake in tariff legislation—and gave $300. Many other Pittsburgh industrialists were not even asked to give; acquaintances explained that it would be useless. They had contributed to the American Iron & Steel Association's fund for other causes. The association's head was no more promising, however much he appreciated Sherman's defense of protected interests. He sent one $200 check and added that he was sure that Conger would be "pleased to learn that we have sent a very liberal supply of tariff tracts into your State."[32]

Contributions came from business *men*, more than from businesses. The distinction is an important one, however far individuals hoped to advance their financial interests, because much of the money came from partisan loyalty and from political aspirations. Gilded Age opinion usually treated businessmen as a separate class from politicians. Liberal reformers spoke of putting politics on a "business basis," and contrasted private efficiency with public incompetence; critics of the Robber Barons treated the titans of industry as outsiders, corrupting the office-seeking classes with bribes and free railroad passes. In fact, the two classes overlapped in a variety of combinations. There were politicians and businessmen, pure and simple, businessmen in politics, and politicians with heavy business investments. Some magnates entered the public arena to protect their investments, others to achieve a recognition of services rendered that only office could give them, and others because they saw their training in financial affairs as the ideal school for a statesmanship that the Gilded Age seemed to lack. For some politicians, business investments were a means to an end, enhancing their power to provide favors to followers or the funds that would make them indispensable to the party. For others, financial connections were a safeguard for that probable day when political power slipped away or a means of sustenance in an era when office, honestly administered, barely paid basic expenses. Rare was that governor or senator who could live on his official salary and still handle the social responsibilities of the position. Finally, of course, for some politicians, official power opened the way to wealth. Speakers of the House met all the right people, and if they wanted to "prove no deadhead" in an enterprise, as James G. Blaine put it, there were plenty of enterprises ready to give them the chance to try.[33]

From such a broad array of monied men, the parties usually could count on large contributions, but the motivation was decidedly mixed. One might look at the roster, certainly incomplete, of great givers to the Democratic campaign fund in 1884: ironmonger William H. Barnum, $27,500; Cooper & Hewitt iron works, $25,300; German newspaper publisher Oswald Ottendorfer, $18,000; banker Daniel Manning, $13,675; city railroad speculator William C. Whitney, $15,250; railroad tycoon James J. Hill, $10,000; coal and railroad executive Arthur Pue Gorman, $14,908.25; and banker Roswell Flower, $16,000. All were businessmen, but except in Hill's case, their primary reason for contribution was no business decision, unless one could describe it as a way of protecting their investment in a political vocation. They did not calculate their donations as money spent to make money, nor, in most cases, did they expect a specific payoff. They were the kind who gave, who always gave, unless the party adopted policies threatening their financial well-being, and even then it must be a threat of the most direct and clear sort.[34]

The Barnums' investment highlights how indispensable funding from professional politicians was. The same list of contributors included Grover Cleveland himself. The presidential candidate was set down for $10,000—the sum that before the nomination he was told would be expected of him if he wanted to run. Any such list on the Republican side would have credited $65,000 to the GOP nominee, James G. Blaine. Nor was this unusual. The spoils system not only fostered the *need* for large amounts of money; it also solved the problem. Indeed, it remained among the most important solutions all the way into the early 1890s.

At the heart of party finance was the principle of assessment on officeholders in particular and partisans in general. In return for being rewarded a place, the loyal partisan was expected to pay some of his or her salary to campaign funds. There might be more than one levy in a year. National, state, county, ward, and district organizations sent out requests. In presidential election years before 1884, the appearance of official party representatives stalking the halls in search of prey was a common sight. No salary was too modest to be overlooked, from municipal scrubwomen to disabled inmates of soldiers' homes and jailhouse wardens.[35]

Reformers put the practice in its bluntest terms, as a highwayman's demand for "your money or your desk." Undoubtedly, an appointee could turn away the assessor and get away with it. Of some hundred thousand federal employees called on for a contribution in 1878, only some 11,500 responded. But that very much depended on the backing of superiors, and that particular year, with a law recently on the books forbidding assessments and the Hayes administration on record against the practice, deskholders may have felt especially safe from dismissal. On the whole, those who refused one assessment were well advised to submit to others, and those who had given in the past were best protected for exercising their discretion thereafter. Over time, press attacks strengthened the resolve of those who resisted demands on themselves, and the efforts of the newly created Civil Service Commission made the collection of unlawful assessments an increasingly risky business.[36]

By setting down the foundations for a merit system and a fixed tenure in national office, the Pendleton Act of 1883 began the movement toward a professional civil service, free from the clamor of the collectors. It could not shut off federal assessments entirely, and it did nothing about the dunning that went on at every other level of government, but even before its passage the biggest individual contributions came not from appointees but from those holding or seeking elective office. No one was immune from the White House to the statehouse. New York city aldermen were taxed $15 to $25 per election precinct. Assemblymen, whose offices had less potential gain, paid $5 to $15. Congressmen paid a little more, but if more than one political organization nominated him, he had to give the same assessment to each one, and there were all kinds of other expenses. Amos Cummings, elected from a New York City district in 1886, found that his nomination required a payment to each assembly district leader, the funds to print 700,000 ballots, a payment for posters and a fee to bill-stickers for plastering them on dry goods boxes and fences and putting them in every barroom and barber shop. "Add to this tickets for balls, Grand Army Posts, church fairs, and target excursions, assessments for banners and transparencies, and the total ran up to fully five thousand dollars," he wrote. And that was in a district where he ran unopposed![37]

The more lucrative or prestigious the office was, the bigger the mulct a party levied on the nominee. A would-be mayor of New York would need to fork over $25,000 to $30,000, a state supreme court justice $20,000, a sheriff or county clerk $10,000, and a district attorney half so much. The more competitive the race, the higher the assessment was likely to be, and as campaign costs rose, so did assessments. New Yorkers could remember a time when Tammany's nominee for sheriff paid a mere $2,000 assessment, just after the Civil War—and that was the same John Kelly who, as boss, is said to have set the price at $25,000.[38]

In many cases, an assessment had all the effect of an entry fee. If it was expected from candidates, they must either be businessmen of some means or have rich friends to back them. Otherwise consideration would be out of the question. Talent, brains, a gift for oratory, social and institutional connections, and influential allies all could overcome the parties' need for funding, and fatheads could not sustain their careers long on a fat bank account. Still, money gave the edge, especially in years when the party was most desperate for funds.

To raise money, managers sought out candidates with a "barrel," or, more precisely, a checkbook that could tide them over until election day. The person selected usually had other merits, and in some cases the money was no more than an incidental advantage. Democrats wanting a presidential candidate in 1876 would have looked closely at any governor of New York, and certainly one with Samuel J. Tilden's savvy. In his well-timed fights on the Tweed Ring and the grafting contractors in New York's upstate Canal Ring, he made himself, in one senator's words, a representative for "the aggressive honesty which is the dominant idea of the time." But his legendary wealth certainly helped. Widely reputed to be "a rich nabob who has made his great wealth out of railroads," Tilden had money to spend against enemies in Ohio and to organize one of the best-constructed campaigns for the nomination in history. Democrats were confident (mistakenly, as it proved) that he would tap his "barrel" liberally to win election.[39]

If wealth was a consideration in the 1876 campaign, it became even more so after Tilden's defeat and what may have been a series of strokes. A virtual prisoner in his home, nearly blind, unable to speak above a whisper, Tilden remained the front-runner for the nomination for eight years, almost to the very day the convention opened. Nostalgia for the one presidential race that Democrats had come closest to winning and resentment at the way Tilden had been deprived of his reputed right to the presidency gave Tilden part of his appeal. The "barrel" did the rest, even among those who saw him as the party's pest. In one editor's words, the Democracy seemed prepared to carry Jonah for the sake of Jonah's "passage-money."[40]

Democrats' selection of a vice presidential nominee in 1880 was even more blatant. To be sure, they needed an Indiana man on the ticket; but there were many favorite sons more prominent that former Congressman William English. Some had warmth, charm, speaking ability, and a popular following. A hard-fisted banker and forecloser, "Ten Per Cent Bill" had none of them. What English did have was money, enough to swing Indiana come October.[41] In 1884, Democrats tried to induce West Virginia's former senator, Henry Gassaway Davis, to accept the vice presidency for the same golden reasons, and twenty years later, when he was in eighties, actually got him to accept.

Vice presidential nominees only reflected a common practice in assigning House seats and settling Senate races. In most states, business leaders could not buy themselves easy preferment. Their rise came after long apprenticeship in different capacities of service to the party. Still, one of those capacities was almost always as the good provider to the campaign war chest in a time of need. In upstate New York, Congressman David Wilber provided just one example. He was president of a national bank and owner of some four thousand acres of cultivated farmland. For many years, he acted as political leader in his county and as an occasional congressman, carrying a Democratic district by a handsome majority after "a campaign noted for its thoroughness and aggressiveness." And its cash—mostly Wilber's. "He is a rough rider in politics," one observer wrote, "and when he is a candidate his trail over the district is a golden blaze." That was more than could be said of the House to which he was elected. Wilber had no talent for public speaking, no gift for making friends, and was often absent. None of these, in so well-heeled a partisan, was a handicap, and the seat was his until he died.[42]

Wealth provided the credentials for national party chairmen and many a working member of national and state committees. For enterprising ways, Ohio had few men to match Arthur Conger. One of Akron's most prominent Republicans, he had begun as a traveling salesman for a manufacturer of mower and reaper blades. By the 1880s, he owned the firm and also was president of plate-glass and window-glass companies, realty firms, tin-plate factories, and a steam-forge concern. He knew wealthy men nationwide and could solicit funds from them with less embarrassment than professional politicians could. A better résumé for political influence could not have been devised. For twenty years, Conger sat on the county, state, and Republican national committees and was a serious prospect for the governorship.[43]

What effect did all this money have on the political process? It did not allow businessmen to dominate the politicians entirely. For party success, many of them were willing to temper their own views, though not so far as to put their business interests into direct peril. Still, the source of campaign funding did shape political life. The assessment process, both on candidates and officeholders, was in effect an informal tax system to sustain the parties. The donors compensated for it out of salaries and fees paid for by the voters at large. Money for public advertising, contracts handed out to anyone but the lowest bidder, added to the costs of governance, and taxpayers picked up the tab.

The usefulness of assessments was one reason why the spoils system, with all its inefficiencies, survived so long. Cities might choose commissions or nonpartisan boards to handle certain city functions, but those most likely to be put on a merit basis were those with not many lucrative rewards attached. Fees from a city clerk's office were tremendous, compared to the rake-off from public libraries or parks. The big moneymakers, the police and fire departments and the post offices, a political organization would try to control as long as possible. The need to repay assessments bred a tacit understanding among hard-eyed party managers that officeholders should be allowed to make what they could from their positions. It assured a police department full of party workers, adding to the campaign war chest a fraction of the take from payoffs and protection money on their beats.

Assessing candidates was not all trickle-down corruption. It left a well-founded impression that offices could be bought, sold, or rented, and discouraged honest men from entering the race. In Rhode Island, the connection between a high office and a fat bankroll became so strong that governorships looked to outsiders like nothing more than a barter.[44] With well-documented cases of "barrel" politics, newspapers readily ascribed corruption to any convention by opponents where a rich man was involved. The more "liberal" the candidate's reputation as a donor to party causes, the more the worst stories were credited. "The money is pouring out in $100 and $200 chunks," one Democratic congressman wrote party leaders about his opponent. "There are regular agents from the East located at the Hotel in the [Disabled Soldiers'] 'Home' whose sole mission is to buy up the inmates." The only complaint among Republicans rose from those who could "hear the heavy thud, accompanied with silvery strains, of the cooperage as it bounds from rock to rock down the hillsides and along the valleys," but could not get their hands on a penny of it.[45]

Could money deflect a party from its mission or divest it of its natural leaders, the professional politicians? Here the answer is not so clear. Much of the agendas that businessmen held dear—of governments friendly to economic promotion and chary about regulation—were so ingrained into politicians of both mainstream parties that no cash transaction was needed. Winning election did not necessarily mean a lasting influence. "Barrel" candidates often made a paltry show in Congress when it came to legislation. Standard Oil money may have elected Henry B. Payne to the Senate, but the seat might as well have been empty for all the influence he wielded, in large part because so many members believed that he had bought his way into their midst; he narrowly escaped expulsion and did not seek a second term. In the House, the greatest leaders were those least involved in business.[142] But certainly wealth gave those who had it an advantage over those who did not in reaching the point where their talents could be tested by experience.[47]

William L. Scott was living proof of that. Representing the Erie, Pennsylvania, district in the 1880s, Scott had entered politics as a congressional page forty years before. He had been elected mayor twice, but, ever since the Civil War, had expanded his political influence by building a fortune, first in railroads, then in coal-land ownership. By 1889, Scott held stock in 22,000 miles of railroads and kept a nationally renowned stable of thoroughbreds. "Scott is a good fellow and means well, never a doubt of that," Daniel Manning, Grover Cleveland's Secretary of the Treasury remarked. That summer, there were even reports that Manning would resign in Scott's favor. He had doubly good reason for gratitude: Scott was staunchly hard-money and spoke eloquently against silver coinage. But Secretary Manning also knew Scott's worth from their dealings when Manning was raising funds for the 1884 presidential campaign. Newspaper estimates put Scott's contribution at $50,000.[48]

But if Scott meant well, he meant especially well for himself. When Democrats were leaning toward a campaign focused on railroad extortions in 1885, Scott was one of the loudest voices against taking on the corporations. He offered cogent reasons, though his own vast holdings could hardly have been far from his mind. Unlike most Pennsylvania politicians, Scott was an outspoken free trader, which took courage. But it did him no financial harm either. Unlike mine owners along the Atlantic seaboard, Scott owned mines that no Nova Scotia coal could undersell. Transport costs across the Appalachians were prohibitive in themselves, and free trade would open up markets for his product across the Great Lakes in Canada, where consumers thought western Pennsylvania coal was a bargain.

Nor could Scott's money muzzle the state party for long, not with so much money from tariff-protected interests lodged on the other side. Only at great cost to the Democratic party could Scott wrest the leadership from Congressman Samuel J. Randall and drive it to endorse tariff reform. The further Scott ranged from where rank-and-file Democrats stood, the more tenuous his hold upon them was. Deprived of administration patronage when President Cleveland lost his bid for a second term, Scott found his money less than sufficient to hold the party in line. The more he concentrated on making a big profit, the more it cost him politically. When Scott moved to crush the mine workers' union during coal-field disturbances in 1889, his Democratic followers fell out of the procession for good. He became such a liability that his announced retirement from politics came as a relief.[49]

The Scotts could never sound the only voice in Democratic counsels, any more than the Wilbers dominated Republican ones. What they could do was to make their viewpoint heard and raise the potential cost for the party in offending them. Ohio Republicans might be willing to risk brewers' contributions to their campaign to satisfy temperance advocates in their party; for winning office, votes counted more than dollars. But it would help tame lawmakers' zeal and make them search for liquor laws likely to affect the distilleries more severely than the breweries, and the two-bit grog shops so popular in Democratic neighborhoods, more than the more respectable bier-gartens in Republican ones. Nor, certainly, was the ability to contribute to party causes the only means that businessmen had of influencing policy and defining lawmakers' agenda. Treated separately from other practices, it seems an inadequate explanation for the business-friendly agendas of the two major parties. Taken in combination with corporations' ability to mount lobbying campaigns, the press's dependence on business advertising, and the range of favors and expertise on special matters that businesses could muster, the preeminence of "barrel" politics helps create a more disturbing picture.

Distraction to the mainstream parties was death to the minor ones. Money may not have been everything. Campaigns could be waged on a shoestring, and with help from nonpolitical institutions— the evangelical churches from which Prohibitionists drew so many of their leaders and so much of their money, or the trade unions and farmers' associations with their own networks of communication to members. Sometimes a third party could compensate for its handicaps. But the very causes for which so many outsiders struggled were never well funded. The business sources that major parties could tap were not just closed to them; the very existence of a Labor party made a powerful incentive for corporations to open their purses to whatever alternative was available. Always the temptation beckoned, of running a candidate who could pay his own way, even if his selection was not quite the perfect fit; always, the major parties could tempt the outsiders into an unofficial alliance, exchanging cash for just the slightest tempering of political conscience. That rough-tongued old political bruiser, Benjamin Butler, might not be a Greenbacker himself in 1884, though he shared the members' faith in the "people's money" and easy credit. But the newly christened People's Party had not just adopted a kindred spirit to lead them. They had adopted a bunting manufacturer and highly paid attorney who, when he ran, paid his own way, and found himself greeting crowds of admirers and fending off mobs of political spongers simultaneously.[50]

The dependence on money only added to the sense of distrust and betrayal that outsiders felt when things went wrong. They were quick to suspect each other's intentions, quick to suspect a sell-out, and to hazard a guess what the purchase price had been. Much of this was the natural paranoia of true believers, fearful of any compromise in the purity of their principles, and insurgents, well aware of all the ways in which the monied major parties could and did use their wealth to skew the process.

But not all. Much of the paranoia had a basis in fact. The Populists, Greenbackers, and others were being bought even when they refused to sell. A minor party had to get its money from somewhere. Often as not, its funds needed to come from Republicans or Democrats, and there were good reasons why the major parties would pay to keep their smaller rivals in business. A Greenback ticket in a Democratic state might draw enough votes away from the majority party to let Republicans come in; a Prohibition ticket just about anywhere was sure to tug far more votes from the Republicans than the Democrats. It was in Democrats' interest to see that those restive with Republicans' halfway measures toward prohibition had an alternative, and that the alternative was well enough fixed to pay for speakers, halls, posters, and, most of all, ballots. It would be an investment well worth it.

So when Republicans charged that the Democrats were financing John P. St. John's presidential campaign in 1884, they believed it, even if the proof was not readily at hand. Indeed, they were quite right. Even more correctly, Democrats alleged that Republican money kept Ben Butler's candidacy in the field, and that its reform agenda had been diverted into a campaign to draw off Democratic votes. Butler had been nominated in May, but he held off his acceptance for three months, until he had assurances of Republican financial backing, and later did not hesitate to insist on the bargains being fulfilled. As the campaign reached its climax, angry letters flew to the Republican national committee leadership, protesting their failure to supply as large a sum as promised. Republicans may have been holding back because they saw quite another need for their money: at that very moment, leading operatives were carrying on negotiations to buy off the Prohibition party candidate and make him retire from the field in their favor. The negotiations fell through, but the stigma of being a "kept" candidate lingered with St. John ever after. So it would always be with insurgent candidates, and the worst of it was that the evidence was so often readily at hand to prove the charge.

Reformers on the fringe like Henry George knew that money's power kept them from reaching the audience their ideas deserved, and knew, too, that inside mainstream party ranks they could never do much more than swell the procession. They had all kinds of remedies. Above all, cheaper campaigns would open the way to candidates of more modest means. Laws forbidding the parades and display that campaigns afforded, an outlawing of the practice of "treating," a ballot officially prepared and distributed, and a series of public halls that at nominal expense could be rented out by the town or city for mass meetings, just as schoolhouses were used in the countryside, would cut away at party expenses. Indeed, George predicted, the parties would be relieved to be spared of most of the burdens: the torchlights and display were done not just to rouse their own voters, but to keep up with the opposition. A law that set the ban on Republican and Democrat alike would be almost welcome.[51]

Aside from the switch to the official "Australian ballot," a reform that the mainstream parties came to appreciate all the more because it freed their funds for other uses, the steps to banish money from politics did not happen. On the contrary, what was happening in the 1880s was politics' own industrial revolution, with the mass production of campaign materials. Parties' administrative machinery was expanding, and so, too, were the lobbies, and one-cause interest groups with exchequers of their own and the power to augment the tracts that parties put out. The Iron and Steel Association, the WCTU, state federations of labor, all had created the networks to engage in politics. Their spending meant that the day of shoestring campaigns was passing, even as the mainstream parties' monopoly on politics and policy began to dim. Those dismayed by the power of money to make policy and politics may have been blessed by their inability to see the future. The song and shout of the parades would fade, but the chink of coin into party coffers had just begun.

University of Kentucky

Notes

1. Z. Fuller to Thomas Jenckes, 28 August 1868, Thomas Jenckes MSS, Library of Congress.
2. *Puck*, 23 January 1889.
3. Henry Ward to Samuel J. Randall, 12 September 1884, Samuel J. Randall MSS, University of Pennsylvania Library; *New York Times*, 2 October 1892. For other wild numbers, see Bangor *Commercial*, 4 September 1884 (which reported allegations of two packages of $50,000 sent to Maine by Democrats); *Cincinnati Enquirer*, 29 September 1884; *Hartford Times*, 20 October, 4 November 1884; *New York Times*, 25 August 1872.
4. For one of the wilder "British gold" stories, see *Bangor Whig and Courier*, 20 November 1884.
5. D. W. Voyles to William E. Chandler, 12 September, 20 October 1868, William E. Chandler MSS, Library of Congress; Fuller to Thomas Jenckes, 11 July 1868, Thomas Jenckes MSS, Library of Congress; George C. Tichenor to John Sherman, 18 September 1880, John Sherman MSS, Library of Congress. Former Senator William Chandler, who had looked over the memorandum books for 1876, knew for a fact that the talk of massive slush funds on the Republican side was wrong. The national committee had spent no more than $150,000 that year, including the legal expenses for the election dispute that followed. But he still believed fabulous tales about the opposition, which, according to his calculation, spent hundreds of thousands of dollars. William E. Chandler to Whitelaw Reid, 1 November 1904, Whitelaw Reid MSS, Library of Congress.
6. Leon Burr Richardson, *William E. Chandler, Republican* (New York, 1940), 96–98; William E. Chandler to Claflin, 16, 21 December, 21 November 1868, 1 January 1869, William C. Claflin MSS, Hayes Presidential Center Library, Fremont. For much higher estimates, see *New York Sun*, 17 November 1888. On the normal cost of a Republican campaign in Ohio ($25,000, and in a presidential year, ideally, $40,000)—and the difficulty raising even that amount—see Charles Foster to Lewis Seasongood, 8 July 1880, Charles Foster Letterbooks, Ohio Historical Society.
7. Irving Katz, *August Belmont: A Political Biography* (New York, 1968), 180–82.
8. For such appeals from Indiana, see George Boutwell, telegram to Wlliam C. Claflin, 2 October 1868, Claflin MSS.
9. James A. Briggs to William C. Claflin, 8 September 1868, Claflin MSS; on Indiana in 1872, see Edwin Morgan to William C. Claflin, 17, 25 September 1872, Claflin MSS; Morgan to Oliver P. Morton, 30 August, 25 September 1872, Edwin D. Morgan MSS, New York State Library; On Pennsylvania in 1872, see Edwin Morgan to William C. Claflin, 21, 25, 27 September, 5 October (telegram), 1872, William E. Chandler to Claflin, 28 August, 24, 28 September, 29, 1872, Morgan and Chandler to Claflin, 26 September 1872 (wire), Russell Errett to Morgan, 13 September 1872, Claflin MSS; Edwin D. Morgan to Jay Cooke, 30 October 1872, Jay Cooke MSS, Historical Society of Pennsylvania, Philadelphia.
10. James G. Blaine to Elihu Washburne, 11 July 1868, John L. Stearns to Washburne, 18 June 1868, Elihu Washburne MSS, Library of Congress; Edwin Morgan to William C. Claflin, 17 August 1872, Claflin MSS. For the $20,000 figure, see Sam Ward to Manton Marble, 13 August 1868, Manton Marble MSS, Library of Congress; for the $15,000 total, see James G. Blaine to Edwin D. Morgan, 10 August 1872, Morgan MSS.
11. John M. Morris to William C. Claflin, 23 September, 20 October 1868, For the southern numbers in 1868, see T. L. Tullock to William C. Claflin, 29 October 1868, William C. Claflin MSS; Tullock to William E. Chandler, 18 Septem-

ber, 13 October 1868, Tullock to Claflin, 30 October 1868, M. A. Southworth to Chandler, 21 October 1868, Chandler MSS.

12. Thomas L. Tullock to William E. Chandler, 13 October 1868, Tullock to Claflin, 30 October 1868, Chandler MSS; William E. Chandler to William C. Claflin, 12 November 1872, Claflin MSS. Tullock's letter suggests that the full $5,000 may not have been delivered. For the later neglect of the South, see A. H. Pettibone to Edward McPherson, 18 September 1884, McPherson MSS. For Indiana's neglect, once it stopped being an "October state," see Robert D. Marcus, *Grand Old Party: Political Structure in the Gilded Age, 1880–1896* (New York, 1971), 96. For a November state's neglect, see Edwin D. Morgan to O. C. Moore, 22 October 1872, Morgan MSS.

13. On congressional races, see William E. Chandler to Jay Cooke, 22 September 1868, Jay Cooke MSS; Alphonso Hart to Edward McPherson, 28 August 1884, A. C. White to McPherson, 8 September 1884, McPherson MSS; Edward Bragg to William Vilas, William Vilas MSS, State Historical Society of Wisconsin.

14. As note, for example, A. H. Conner to William E. Chandler, 17 October 1868, Chandler MSS; Marcus, *Grand Old Party,* 48–49; James G. Blaine to Edwin D. Morgan, 10 August 1872, Morgan MSS.

15. Edwin D. Morgan to Henry D. Cooke, 4 October 1872, Morgan MSS; Edward McPherson to John Roach, 2 February 1885, McPherson MSS.

16. William E. Chandler to William C. Claflin, 20 November 1868, Claflin MSS.

17. *Detroit Free Press,* 17 September 1886; *Cincinnati Enquirer,* 1 February 1881; Joseph R. Hawley to Edwin D. Morgan, 1 September 1872, Morgan MSS; Benjamin F. Whittemore to William Claflin, 7 September 1868, A. J. Wright to J. M. S. Williams, 16 December 1868, Claflin MSS.

18. Katz, *August Belmont,* 176–77; J. B. Chaffee to Edward McPherson, 8 October 1884, McPherson MSS; J. C. F. Beyland to William E. Chandler, 30 August 1884, Chandler MSS; *New York Times,* 24 August 1884 (humor magazine). On the Cincinnati German press, see Richardson, *William E. Chandler,* 148–49; Edwin Morgan to William C. Claflin, 21, 23, 27 September 1872, Claflin MSS; Cincinnati *Gazette,* 14, 30 September, 2 October 1872.

19. John W. Forney to William Claflin, 20 August 1871; R. M. Kelly to William Claflin, 7 August 1871, Claflin MSS.

20. For other southern newspapers seeking Republican national committee funding, see John M. Morris to Claflin, 23 September, 20 October, 15 December 1868, 20 January, 16 February 1869, William E. Chandler to Claflin, 19 December 1868 (*Charleston Republican*); Stewart L. Woodford to Claflin, 24 November 1868, A. P. Ketchum to John E. Hayes, 28 April 1866, E. W. Clark, Jay Cooke et al., subscription agreement, 21 September 1866 (*Savannah National Republican*); William E. Chandler to Claflin, 22 January 1870, James J. S. Spelman to Claflin, 23 February 1869, Claflin MSS.

21. *New York Herald,* 1 November 1882, 2 November 1884; *New York Sun,* 31 October 1886.

22. Thomas M. Kelly to Samuel J. Randall, 18 October 1880, Randall MSS (tax receipts); *New York Standard,* 3 November 1888 (tax receipts); F. A. Healy to Wendell Anderson, 11 October 1876, Wendell Anderson MSS, State Historical Society of Wisconsin; Charles St. J. Collis to Elihu Washburne, 13 November 1868, Washburne MSS (naturalization papers).

23. *New York Standard,* 10 April 1888. For vote-buying in Indiana in 1888, see Walter Q. Gresham to Noble C. Butler, 30 October 1888, Noble C. Butler MSS, Indiana Historical Society.

24. A Pennsylvanian, "The Ills of Pennsylvania," *Atlantic,* 88 (October 1901), 562; U. S. Trammell to John C. Houk, 29 October 1894, Houk Family MSS, McClung Library, Knoxville.

25. Edgar J. Levey, "An Election in New York," *North American Review* 145 (December 1887): 681; *New York Standard* (21 April 1888); Henry George, "Money in Elections," *North American Review* 136 (February 1883): 202; *New York Sun*, 25 November 1888; Thomas E. Will, "Political Corruption: How Best Oppose?" *Arena* 10 (November 1894): 848; David A. Biggs to John C. Houk, 22 October 1894, L. R. Carden to John C. Houk, 28 October 1894, Houk Family MSS; "M. C.," *Nation*, 18 November 1880; *New York Sun*, 11 December 1884; S. B. Chase to Luman H. Weller, 6 November 1884, W. R. Mead to Weller, 12 November 1884, Luman H. Weller MSS, State Historical Society of Wisconsin; Concord *Labor Reform Dispatch*, 11 February 1870.

26. Richardson, *William E. Chandler*, 112–13; James A. Briggs to William C. Claflin, 8 September 1868, Carl Schurz to Claflin, 2 August 1868, Claflin MSS.

27. John M. Forbes to William C. Claflin, 2, 23 August, 17, 24 September 1872, William E. Chandler to William C. Claflin, 24 September 1872, Claflin MSS; George F. Dawson to John A. Logan, 8 October 1884, John A. Logan MSS, Library of Congress. The idea of assessing all government bondholders and national banks had been around at least since 1868. See Richardson, *William E. Chandler*, 97–98.

28. For the balkiness of corporations, see, for instance, William E. Chandler to Whitelaw Reid, 1 November 1904, Whitelaw Reid MSS, Library of Congress. For contributions, all individual, see A. T. Stewart to William C. Claflin, 29 September 1868, William E. Chandler list of subscriptions into the Republican national committee, n.d., but clearly 1868, Claflin MSS; William R. Grace to R. B. Minturn, 8 October 1884, Grace to J. S. Coleman, 8 October 1884, William R. Grace MSS, Columbia University.

29. James S. Clarkson to James G. Blaine, 26 June 1884, James G. Blaine MSS, Library of Congress; P. E. Chapin to Arthur L. Conger, 5 October 1885, Arthur L. Conger MSS, Hayes Presidential Center Library.

30. James A. Kehl, *Boss Rule in the Gilded Age: Matt Quay of Pennsylvania* (Pittsburgh, 1981), 98; James G. Blaine to Whitelaw Reid, 26 January 1888, Reid MSS; for other private complaints, see A. London Sowdue to Edward McPherson, 27 August 1884, Edward McPherson MSS, Library of Congress.

31. John Sherman to Arthur L. Conger, 15 September, 15 December 1885, Asa S. Bushnell to Conger, 16, 18 September 1885, Conger MSS.

32. Samuel Thomas to Arthur L. Conger, 24 September 1885, C. W. Moulton to Conger, 3 October 1885, W. S. King to Conger, 21 September 1885, Hussey, Howe & Company to Conger, 23 September 1885, William G. Park to Conger, 23 September 1885, James M. Swank to Conger, 23 September, 6 October 1885, Conger MSS.

33. Marcus, *Grand Old Party*, 66–67, 134–36.

34. Mark D. Hirsch, *William C. Whitney, Modern Warwick* (New York, 1948), 238–39. For Whitney's contributions in 1884, see Charles J. Canda to William C. Whitney, 4, 24, 31 October, 11 November 1884, William C. Whitney MSS, Library of Congress.

35. Richardson, *William E. Chandler*, 98–100; Dorman B. Eaton, "Political Assessments," *North American Review* 135 (September 1882): 197–201; *Indianapolis News*, 3 November 1884.

36. Marcus, *Grand Old Party*, 86–87, 178–79; Whitelaw Reid to James G. Blaine, 18 October 1884, Reid MSS; Joseph Cannon to Edward McPherson, 29 July 1884, Edward McPherson MSS; *New York Evening Post*, 15 September 1884; *Bangor Commercial*, 25 August 1884; James S. Clarkson to E. Halford, 23 April 1892, Benjamin Harrison MSS, Library of Congress.

37. *New York Times*, 24 August, 27 September 1884; Ivins, *Machine Politics*, 55; "A Congressman's Reveries," *New York Sun*, 18 November 1888.

38. Ivins, *Machine Politics*, 54–58, 65–67; *New York Standard*, 20 October 1888, 5 January 1889; "A Millionaire Senate," *Harper's Weekly*, 30 November 1889, 951.

39. A. T. Glaze to William A. Anderson, 17 June 1876, Anderson MSS; *Cincinnati Enquirer*, 22 June 1876; Eugene Casserly to Manton Marble, 26 November 1874, S. L. M. Barlow to Marble, 16 August 1886, Marble MSS.

40. Alexander I. P. Garesche to Rodmond Gibbons, 14 November 1879, Thomas F. Bayard MSS, Library of Congress; S. L. M. Barlow to Manton Marble, 16 August 1886, Marble MSS; *Puck*, 7 April 1880, 70 (quote); 12 May 1880, 162; 26 May 1880, 200.

41. *Irish World and American Industrial Liberator*, 7 August 1880; *Chattanooga Daily Times*, 16 October 1880; *Puck*, 22 September 1880, 34; 13 October 1880, 84.

42. *Memorial Addresses on the Life and Character of David Wilber*, 51st Cong., 1st sess. (Washington, D.C., 1890), 3–4, 8; *New York Herald*, 9, 19 October 1886; Walter H. Bunn to Daniel Lamont, 21 October 1886, Grover Cleveland MSS, Library of Congress; *New York Times*, 7 October 1888.

43. Katz, *August Belmont*, 175–77; *National Cyclopaedia of American Biography*, 2:206–7.

44. "Rhode Island," *Harper's Weekly*, 21 April 1888, 278; *St. Louis Post-Dispatch*, 10 March 1887.

45. John A. McMahon to Samuel J. Randall, 12 September 1880, Randall MSS; *Cincinnati Enquirer*, 22, 30 July, 7 August 1880.

46. *Chicago Tribune*, 9 July 1884.

47. "A Free Vote for New York," *Harper's Weekly*, 26 May 1888, 371; *Puck*, 2 April 1884, 66.

48. J. J. Faran to William Allen, 27 October 1876, William Allen MSS, Library of Congress; Daniel Manning to Manton Marble, 9 March 1886, Marble MSS; Philadephia *Record*, 15 June, 12 July 1886, 21 September 1891 (obituary); Lewis R. Rathgeber, "The Democratic Party in Pennsylvania, 1880–1896," Ph.D. diss., University of Pittsburgh, 1885, 133.

49. Philadelphia *Record*, 8, 11, 14 August 1886; Rathgeber, "Democratic Party in Pennsylvania," 144.

50. *John Swinton's Paper*, 25 May, 1 June, 12 July 1884, 14 June 1885.

51. Henry George, "Money in Elections," *North American Review* 136 (February 1883): 206–9.

JULIAN E. ZELIZER

Seeds of Cynicism: The Struggle over Campaign Finance, 1956–1974

"It is a cesspool, it is a source of infection for the body politic," Senator Hubert Humphrey (D-Minn.) warned his fellow senators in 1973 about the private financing of elections. "[I]f it doesn't stop, there are going to be good men in this hall right here today who are going down the drain, not that you are guilty, not that you have done anything wrong, but that the public is disenchanted with all of us, and they are going to want somebody new and say I want a fresh one here."[1] From 1971 through President Nixon's resignation in 1974, Congress enacted the boldest campaign finance reforms in American history, including strong disclosure laws, public financing for presidential elections, contribution and spending limits, and an independent enforcement commission. Despite these reforms, after only a decade under the new laws, citizens still felt that campaign finance was corrupt.

Campaign finance is one of the most vexing problems in American democracy. To achieve reform, proponents must convince incumbent politicians to change a system in which they have succeeded. To make matters more difficult, campaign finance reform

The University at Albany, the Carl Albert Center, the Dirksen Congressional Research Center, and the Gerald Ford Foundation generously provided grants that funded this research. The following are the collections and abbreviations used for this article: Carl Albert Center, Norman, Oklahoma (CAC); Common Cause Papers, Princeton, New Jersey (CCP); Papers of the Democratic National Committee, Washington, D.C. (DNCP); Papers of the Democratic Study Group, Washington, D.C. (DSGP); George Meany Archives, Silver Spring, Maryland (GMA); Gerald Ford Presidential Library, Ann Arbor, Michigan (GFL); James O'Hara Papers, Ann Arbor, Michigan (JOP); John F. Kennedy Presidential Library, Boston, Massachusetts (JFKL); Lyndon B. Johnson Presidential Library, Austin, Texas (LBJL); Mike Mansfield Papers, Missoula, Montana (MMP); Richard Nixon Papers, College Park, Maryland (RNP).

has never been driven by strong electoral pressure. The laws that passed in the early 1970s provide policy historians an opportunity to contribute to current debates about reforming the ties between money and politics.

In studying the 1970s reforms, the first puzzle historians must solve is how campaign finance reform passed despite enormous political opposition and lukewarm public support.[2] Although most accounts stress Watergate, this study suggests that a more complex intersection of events culminated in reform. By placing less explanatory weight on the Watergate scandal to evaluate the 1974 legislation, this essay stresses how antecedent political events created a window of opportunity for reformers at the same time that prior decisions limited the long-term impact of their accomplishments.[3]

In the 1960s, campaign finance reform did not emerge because of intense electoral pressure but, rather, emanated from a reform coalition that was neither a grassroots movement nor a group of elites at the center of political power. Rather, these were political actors operating at the margins of power who believed that representative government could be improved. The coalition, composed of legislators, experts, philanthropists, foundations, and public interest groups, was at the heart of the struggle over campaign finance. Members of this coalition claimed that substantive institutional reform was essential to restore public trust in democratic politics. Refusing to believe that politicians would independently monitor or cleanse their own institutions, the coalition supported a number of reforms in the political process ranging from the codification of ethics to the creation of an independent prosecutor. Campaign finance always maintained the most tenuous position of all the reforms (compared to filibuster reform, for example) since it touched on every interest in the political system, including legislators who were supportive of process reform. Still, the coalition was able to place campaign finance reform on the national agenda even without widespread public interest or support.[4]

But the efforts of this coalition were not sufficient for reform to pass.[5] Even without strong public pressure, politicians in the 1960s developed a self-interest in campaign finance reform as a result of escalating television costs and the evolving financial condition of the parties. A new adversarial media, moreover, created the perception that opposing campaign finance reform could be politically dangerous. These forces produced the political interest needed to make reform viable. Politicians then restructured the coalition's proposals to satisfy their own needs. Watergate created political support for reforms as legislators feared an angry constituency prepared to remove them from office. But scandal did not automatically produce reform. When Watergate occurred, the coalition was in place to take advantage of the favorable climate and additional conditions had created an interest for politicians.

The second puzzle historians must resolve is why reform failed to end public distrust of campaigns. Most accounts have focused on events after the passage of the 1974 legislation that undermined the reforms, ranging from the law of unintended consequences, to Supreme Court decisions, to the permanent power of special interest groups. While these factors are certainly important, this essay emphasizes critical choices and problems that reformers made before 1974. During the incubation period between 1956 and 1970, the coalition struggled to define how the debate would be framed.[6] The choices made during these years limited the ultimate impact of the reforms. Most important, the coalition left intact most of the underlying pressures on campaign finance. For example, they did not tackle the declining importance of political parties, leaving high-cost television as the principle medium of political communication. Although parties regained some importance in the 1990s, they served primarily as another source of campaign contributions for individual candidates rather than dominant forces of political communication, a function they had once served. Moreover, even with the substantial legislation that passed, the coalition made debilitating compromises, such as accepting political action committees (PACs) and limiting public financing of campaigns.

The most striking failure of the coalition was their inability to build sustained grassroots support for this issue. The major parties supported campaign finance reform only when there was extreme internal financial pressure to do so. With limited electoral support, both parties immediately turned away from reform once it no longer served their interest. As a result of its weak electoral support, opponents were able to water down proposals or undermine laws after they passed. Key opponents of reform were rarely voted out of office because of their opposition to campaign finance. The leading opponent, Wayne Hays (D-Ohio), lost his power because of a notorious sex scandal, not because of his determined efforts to gut campaign finance laws. The coalition never obtained the popular support for the kinds of expansive government intervention, such as full government subsidies for all federal campaigns and free advertising, that was necessary to tame permanently the candidate-centered election system.

The Pressures on Campaign Finance

Federal campaign finance laws originated in the Progressive Era. In 1907, Congress passed legislation that prohibited corporations and national banks from contributing to candidates in federal elections. This prohibition grew out of the belief that large contributions inherently corrupted politics. Reformers also believed it to be undemocratic for large organizations to use compulsory funds without the consent of contributors.[7] At this time, however, Congress rejected a proposal to finance presidential campaigns publicly. Instead, Congress required interstate party committees and congressional campaign committees to disclose campaign receipts only *after* the election, thereby diluting the effect of this reform. Nor did the laws apply to committees operating within a single state (designated "single-state committees"). In 1911, Congress strengthened the disclosure requirements for the House and Senate and imposed spending limits. Congress again endorsed these provisions in 1925 by mandating federal regulation in all elections except in state primaries in accordance with a 1921 Supreme Court decision that ruled the federal government could not regulate state primaries.

The Progressive Era reforms had a negligible effect. Candidates easily found loopholes to evade unenforced regulations. Given the Supreme Court decision to limit federal regulation in the states, primary spending increased, obliterating the effects of reform in southern states. In addition, single-state committees were unregulated. Union contributions were also the source of great controversy. The Congress of Industrial Organizations (CIO) created the first political action committee in 1943 to support Democratic candidates.[8] Although the CIO first used general treasury funds, the union soon turned to voluntary $1 contributions from members. In 1947, following widely publicized congressional investigations into the CIO's influence in the 1944 and 1946 elections, Congress made permanent wartime prohibitions on union usage of general funds for campaigns. The right of unions to collect voluntary donations for campaign contributions remained contentious. Meanwhile, state-level initiatives foundered. Politicians underreported contributions, politicians withheld information from the public, and corruption survived even in state systems with public financing (Puerto Rico). With minimal reform, campaign finance changed very little.

During the post–World War II period, the Progressive Era laws failed to eliminate the four underlying factors that generated the strong incentives for candidates to seek private money. One was the declining organizational strength of parties. Unlike the nineteenth century, parties were no longer the primary vehicle for communicating issues or mobilizing voters during presidential and congressional campaigns. The organizational basis of parties weakened significantly throughout the century due to several factors, including Progressive Era reforms. Candidates began to communicate to voters through the media and professional campaign specialists rather than through the parties. The television "spot" became a main vehicle for candidates to communicate to the public, along with television news programs and newspapers, in the same fashion as the nineteenth-century party parade, picnic, and newspaper. Parties, which had previously been dominant, became the instrument of candidates. The second factor was the increase in campaign costs. As politicians used the radio and then television to communicate with voters, campaign costs rose dramatically for individual candidates. Third, there was little public pressure to reform campaign finance. Even though voters complained to pollsters that money corrupted politics, there was no substantive electoral pressure to change the system or to punish those who opposed reform legislation. Finally, the constitutional protection of free speech made it difficult to impose substantive restrictions on campaign spending.[9] Although it was unclear until 1976 how the Supreme Court would view legislation enforcing campaign spending limits, they gave indications in the 1950s and 1960s that they would deem them illegitimate.[10]

These four factors—weak parties, rising campaign costs, limited public pressure for reform, and the constitutional protection of free speech—shaped campaign finance for most of the period that followed the New Deal. But between 1956 and 1973, the convergence of several interdependent forces elevated the problems of this campaign system to the forefront of the political agenda as a reform coalition formed. As a result, tensions over campaign finance reached a boiling point when President Nixon began his second term in office.

The Reemergence of Reform, 1956–1964

Between 1956 and 1963, a small group of legislators realized that the Progressive Era campaign reforms were ineffective. Although each reformer had a different objective, most supported improved disclosure regulations in addition to tax incentives to encourage small contributions. Liberal Democrats such as Senators Albert Gore (D-Tenn.) and Thomas Hennings (D-Mo.) hoped to constrain large contributors, limit corruption, and end the secrecy surrounding elections. Conservatives John McClellan (D-Ariz.) and Barry Goldwater (R-Ariz.) used reform to attack organized labor. Although neither faction was able to pass legislation, their efforts caused two key factions to solidify their position. Organized labor emerged as the lead opponent of regulating PACs. Campaign finance experts became the external voice promoting reform.

In 1956, a congressional scandal involving campaign finance received national attention. On February 3, Senator Francis Case (R-S.D.) admitted that he had been offered cash by an oil company in exchange for supporting legislation. Although Case rejected the payment, the admission led President Dwight Eisenhower to veto the bill in question to avoid any appearance of corruption. The scandal increased congressional interest in the issue of campaign finance. Gore, for example, headed an investigation through the Privileges and Election Subcommittee of the Senate Rules Committee. The senator hired University of North Carolina Professor Alexander Heard, the leading expert on campaign finance and author of the landmark publication *The Cost of Democracy*, to serve as a consultant to the staff. Heard recruited Herbert Alexander, a newly minted political scientist from Yale. The committee produced an extensive analysis of campaign contributions. Soon after, John McClellan's Special Committee to Investigate Political Activities, Lobbying, and Campaign Contributions focused on labor's political activities. However, no legislation passed.

While legislation did not pass, these investigations put labor on the defensive. Organized labor felt that its political standing, only recently secured during the New Deal and World War II, was under attack from big business and conservatives in government. During the late 1950s, the government investigated union corruption. The National Association of Manufacturers was conducting a national anti-union campaign. In this context, union leaders perceived campaign finance reform as a tool for conservatives to emasculate their political power. Labor contributions were generally funneled through political action committees. When the American Federation of Labor (AFL) and CIO merged in 1955, leaders created the Committee on Political Education (COPE) to influence elections.[11] To avoid legal violations, COPE used voluntary member contributions deposited in a segregated account for cash contributions to candidates.

Drawing on general AFL-CIO funds in addition to the voluntary contributions, COPE used these dollars for "political education." Unions could use compulsory dues for indirect expenditures such as providing campaign volunteers and publications about candidates. By 1956, there were 17 national union and 155 state and local affiliate political action committees.[12] Some unions also illegally directed union funds toward campaigns.

For these reasons, union leaders opposed PAC regulations. At this time, wealthy contributors known as "fat cats" were the main contributors to parties and candidates. They did not use formal PACs. Thus, PACs offered unions a counterweight to these contributors. By pooling contributions, unions created a lobbying presence and obtained access to politicians in a way that workers could never achieve individually. Since corporations were barred from making direct donations to candidates, corporate officials and their families contributed as individuals. Sometimes corporations illicitly concealed the source of donations through law firms. Unknown to the public, many corporations also maintained PAC-like operations without public knowledge: Gulf Oil, Union Carbide, McDonnell Douglas, Ford Motors, and General Electric had solicited executives and distributed the money to candidates since the 1950s.[13] Corporations often gave executives bonuses or inflated salaries with the implicit agreement that the money would be returned for campaign contributions.[14] Because the Justice Department ignored the Progressive Era laws, these activities went unpunished.

Unions argued that conservatives such as Senator Goldwater were using reform to combat labor's political power without doing anything about these corporate contributions.[15] Conservatives regularly proposed amendments that specifically targeted labor's committees. Regarding 1959 legislation, AFL-CIO Vice President Walter Reuther wrote President George Meany: "What little meaning the Bill has is aimed at labor and other liberal groups; if turned loose on the Senate floor in the present atmosphere, we would be faced with the strong probability that anti-labor forces in both parties would make an all out effort to amend the Bill so as to block and if possible prohibit all political activity by labor."[16] Labor continued through the 1970s to lobby against those who supported regulations on its committees.

Besides labor, another group that responded to campaign finance reform between 1956 and 1964 was composed of campaign finance experts. In an age when this issue generated little public interest and there was no major scandal to keep it at the forefront of public attention, these experts created a permanent constituency for reform and monitored campaigns in lieu of government enforcement. They would remain at the center of the reform coalition. Their efforts originated with William Vanderbilt, former governor of Rhode Island, who established the Committee on Campaign Contributions and Expenditures in January 1958. The committee included economist Seymour Harris, Eleanor Roosevelt, businessman Paul Hoffman, Harvard University Professor of Law Milton Katz, and President of Columbia University Grayson Kirk.[17] Even George Meany joined since it was good from the "standpoint of public relations."[18] The committee endorsed disclosure, centralized campaign committees, contribution limits, tax deductions for small contributors, and extending reforms to primaries.

Disclosure was the committee's most desired goal. At this time, there were virtually no data available on who contributed to campaigns or how campaign financing even worked. Information about the existing campaign finance system, in the minds of these experts and philanthropists, was the most important reform, as it could enable voters to make informed decisions. They assumed that voters would punish those who abused the laws. As the committee argued: "Full publicity is a key factor for there may well be no better test of propriety of a contribution or expenditure than the willingness to expose it to general public knowledge. It would also enable our citizens to know what the facts really are and to base plans for improvement on these facts, rather than guess and rumor."[19] Vanderbilt appointed Herbert Alexander, from Gore's investigations, to direct a research division that would analyze existing data and disseminate that data to the public through the media. The committee was renamed the Citizen's Research Foundation.

Information was difficult to obtain. Armed only with limited funds and a small staff, Alexander rummaged through the files of the Clerk of the House and Secretary of the Senate. The data were notoriously unreliable. To avoid interstate committee reporting requirements, candidates maintained campaign committees in one state. Single-state committees were immune from investigation. Even information from interstate committees often went unreported. To make matters worse, Alexander could not bring typewriters or adding machines into the Clerk's office, nor could he make photocopies.[20] In spite of these difficulties, Alexander found information by gathering what he could and drawing on information compiled by the Washington-based publication, *Congressional Quarterly*. Based on his research, the Citizens' Research Foundation released several studies of campaigns. One of its first major publications provided an unprecedented look into how the Democrats financed the 1960 presidential campaign.[21]

As president, Kennedy brought these campaign finance experts into the executive branch when he invited Alexander Heard to lead a Commission on Campaign Costs. Heard then hired Herbert Alexander to direct the staff. The White House insisted that its goal was to curtail big contributors, not to replace privately financed campaigns with public finance.[22] The 1962 commission report stressed the need to reduce the role of large donors through tax incentives for small contributors. At the same time, the commission said it was essential to minimize campaign costs and establish an independent commission to publicize data. Finally, they dismissed spending limits as ineffective and instead supported full disclosure.[23] Based on Heard's recommendations, Kennedy retained Alexander to lobby for a tax incentive.[24] But Congress rejected the measure; fiscal conservatives and tax reformers complained it cost too much, while liberals attacked it as regressive.

When Lyndon Johnson became president in 1963, he closed Alexander's operation and canceled a White House conference on the issue. Besides Johnson's lack of interest in reform, the Department of Justice challenged Kennedy's commission as being divorced from political reality. One official warned that if the government "scientifically" identified techniques to reduce costs, as the commission suggested, managers would spend the savings elsewhere.[25] Clearly not welcomed by Johnson, Alexander left the administration and returned to the Citizen's Research Foundation, where he received grants from the Ford and Carnegie Foundations to write case studies on campaigns. His work continued to receive media attention.

As a result of the Case bribery scandal and the events it triggered, two vital interests in this battle had emerged. On the one hand, labor developed a hostile stand toward regulation of political action committees. On the other hand, campaign finance experts supported by philanthropists and foundations devoted themselves to the production of knowledge on campaign costs. If the government would not provide reliable information on elections, the experts would privately supply research and the media would publicize their findings. Failing to produce legislation, these experts built momentum for future efforts and helped define a policy agenda.

Television, Parties, and Scandal, 1964–1969

This cadre of experts and legislators in the reform coalition were not enough to sustain support for reform. Although Johnson dismissed campaign reform during his first years in office, external forces drove the issue to national attention. Skyrocketing television costs placed extraordinary pressure on politicians to secure funds. The evolving financial structure of the parties triggered Republican and Democratic interest in reform. Finally, a series of scandals before Watergate led reporters and politicians to focus on this issue.

Television drove up campaign costs to unprecedented levels. As the traditional role of parties continued to decline, candidates relied increasingly on television "spots" to sell themselves in elections. Television did not have a discernable financial impact in the 1950s when campaign costs rose only at the rate of inflation.[26] The effects of television on campaigns were striking and became a subject of constant discussion. More campaigning took place through advertising rather than parties. The Citizens' Research Foundation reported that election spending in 1968 was 25 percent higher than 1964.[27] In 1956, each vote cast cost 19 cents, while by 1968 that figure had risen to 56 cents.[28] Politicians faced significant pressure to obtain enough funds.

The parties responded with different financial strategies. Republicans supplemented their traditional large donors by broadening their contributor base to conservative groups and individual citizens. Conservative campaign specialist Richard Viguerie mastered the use of direct mail. He went to the files of the Clerk of the House to see who had donated more than $50 to conservative candidates. Using computers, he then sent out personalized mail to those supporters requesting small donations. In 1964, as a result of these mailings, individual citizens and single-issue groups funded much of Goldwater's presidential campaign. The senator had received 380,000 responses to direct mail with contributions of $100 each.[29] Given their broad support base and reliance on informal corporate contributions, Republicans endorsed incentives for small contributors and allied with southern Democrats to support the regulation of PACs.

Since they controlled the presidency and Congress, Democrats felt less pressure to innovate in the 1960s, even though the party had accumulated astronomical debt. Democrats also stayed with their old tactics by leaning more on large contributors. Non-southern congressional incumbents continued their reliance on labor and liberal organizations. In 1961, Democrats launched the President's Club, where members made donations in exchange for invitations to monthly events with prominent officials, including the president. There were more than 4,400 President's Club members by 1965.[30] The Democrats raised money through corporate advertising books for conventions. Without supporting candidates, corporations pur-chased tax-deductible ads. In 1964, the party produced a $15,000-a-page advertising book. Republicans copied this method, although not as effectively, since they were in the minority. While Democrats expanded their small contributor drive in 1966, these efforts were ancillary.[31] With Democrats in the White House and labor control-ling PACs, this plan worked. But after Richard Nixon's victory in 1968, large contributors turned away from the party. Republicans also started to benefit from the PACs formed by the American Medi-cal Association in 1961 and NAM in 1963. This change would lead more mainstream Democrats to support public financing and cam-paign regulations.

The third major development involved an increasingly aggres-sive news media that uncovered a series of 1960s scandals involving campaign finance. One involved Senator Thomas Dodd, a promi-nent senior Democrat from Connecticut. In their nationally syndi-cated column, Drew Pearson and Jack Anderson revealed the senator's illicit activities such as Dodd's use of campaign money for personal purposes. The Senate censured Dodd on June 23, 1967. In reporting the story, the papers detailed how Dodd raised money from wealthy individuals at "testimonial dinners" where politicians spoke to crowds paying $100 a plate. The dramatic scandal, which unfolded on the front pages of newspapers and magazines, produced extensive coverage into unregulated campaign practices.[32]

Democratic fund-raising tactics were the center of attention in 1965 and 1966. Republicans revealed how Democrats solicited funds from corporate executives with large military contracts. The charges were based on information from the Citizens' Research Foundation and *Congressional Quarterly*. In response to this scandal, Senator John Williams (R-Del.) successfully added an amendment to 1966 tax leg-islation which eliminated the deduction businesses received for the contributions. In addition to this disincentive, many companies stopped donating because they were being "badgered by reporters" about why they had contributed to Democrats and "what they were promised in return."[33] Notwithstanding the scandals, Democrats still courted large contributors. For example, the Democrats held a $500-a-plate dinner with organizers and simply refrained from using the term "President's Club."[34]

Public opinion polls reflected contradictory attitudes toward campaign reform in the late 1960s. On the one hand, a majority of those polled favored limits on the total amount of money that candidates for federal office could spend. Yet Americans rarely demonstrated strong support for alternative forms of campaign finance. In 1956, only 31 percent of Americans said they would donate $5 to the party of their choice; 50 percent said they would not. Twelve years later, not more than 49 percent responded that they would make a donation to the party of their choice, while opposition still hovered at 50 percent.[35] Nor was government the answer. A 1964 poll found 71 percent of those surveyed were opposed to publicly financed presidential campaigns.[36] In this period, Americans never rated campaign reform as a key problem.

With Republicans attacking Democratic fund-raising tactics, President Johnson called on Congress in May 1966 to extend disclosure laws into primary and general elections and to create a tax deduction for contributions up to $100. However, the president refrained from supporting an independent commission. He told Congress that it was time for a change since "we have tolerated the growth of seeds of cynicism from the underbrush surrounding our present methods of financing political campaigns."[37] Senator Joseph Clark (D-Pa.) attempted unsuccessfully to move Johnson's proposals forward. He encountered hostility on almost every measure and received weak support from the administration. The Senate Rules and Administration Committee passed a watered-down version of the bill written by Senator Cannon's (D-Nev.) Privileges and Elections Subcommittee. In the House, Robert Ashmore (D-S.C.), chair of the Subcommittee on Elections in the House Administration committee, and Republican Charles Goodell (R-N.Y.) introduced a stronger measure (drafted by Herbert Alexander) that expanded disclosure, established an independent commission, ended spending limits, and prevented unions and corporations from using voluntary contributions for political expenditures. Although the subcommittee reported a bill on October 3, Chairman Omar Burleson's (D-Tex.) House Administration Committee killed the legislation.

In 1966, Congress passed a direct subsidy for presidential elections as an alternative to Johnson's proposal. Senator Russell Long (D-La.) proposed an amendment in June, along with Senators Nelson,

Metcalf, and Douglas, to establish a Presidential Campaign Fund. The measure for the first time introduced public finance into presidential elections without imposing any contribution or spending restrictions. Wilbur Mills (D-Ark.), chair of the House Ways and Means Committee, surprised colleagues by accepting a provision he previously opposed as too costly. Long favored a subsidy over tax incentives as more progressive, but a direct appropriation was unacceptable politically.[38] Therefore, Long proposed a tax checkoff where individuals could allocate a dollar of taxes. Money would go to the major parties; minor parties qualified by obtaining four million votes. This subsidy soon came under fire. Senator Williams attacked it as too expensive, while Gore warned that third parties would be crippled. Without barring spending limits, he added, the subsidy was just a boon to the parties. Despite this criticism, Congress passed the legislation and for the first time subsidized elections. Johnson signed the legislation into law.

Behind closed doors, as Congress passed the direct subsidy, President Johnson formed a task force in September 1966 under the direction of Harvard University's Richard Neustadt. Neustadt worked with Heard, then the chancellor of Vanderbilt University, and Malcolm Moos of the Ford Foundation, a former political scientist at Johns Hopkins University and former assistant to President Eisenhower. At first, the group was charged with reexamining old proposals. But the passage of Long's campaign fund changed the task force's agenda to protecting public subsidies from being attacked as a "grab-bag" for incumbents. The task force discovered that many politicians and experts opposed public subsidies for elections, instead favoring incentives for small contributions.[39] Heard, for example, warned that there were "great dangers" in the federal subsidy relating to the "voluntary character" of political activities in America. He also worried about the effect of "bureaucratic rigidities" on parties. Another member warned that "creating a beast which won't work will add to the already great cynicism over political financing."[40] Senator Robert Kennedy (D-N.Y.) acknowledged that direct subsidies promoted the centralization of political power and raised constitutional problems by curtailing freedom of speech by requiring contribution and spending limits. Public subsidies, he said, were antithetical to the tradition of individual participation.[41] Politically, Mills told the task force that Congress would never vote for the extension of subsidies to the legislative branch since that would "finance the opponents of Congressional incumbents."[42] Hostility toward public finance became clear when Congress rendered Long's program ineffective in May 1967. After a bitter struggle, Gore was able to delay the implementation of the direct subsidy until technical guidelines were determined. This indefinite delay made the fund inoperative.

The month Congress short-circuited Long's campaign fund, Johnson proposed an Election Reform Act that included direct appropriations for presidential elections, regulations on primaries, and disclosure laws for all political committees spending more than $1,000. The administration believed that it had the legislative support to obtain a compromise on these issues based on a headcount that Treasury made of the Senate Finance Committee. Johnson made a speech in which he said that there was more "loophole than law" in campaign finance. Key members of the administration were skeptical about free airtime from the networks since it might not be in the interest of the Democratic party. The networks would only finance public-service appearances or debates, but not finance the crucial type of "spot announcements" that Goldwater had used so effectively in 1964. Moreover, presidential aide Joseph Barr was concerned that free airtime would benefit third-party candidates such as George Wallace.[43] Clark Clifford, who did not believe any legislation would pass in the end because of the free speech problems raised by contribution limitations, suggested that the president promote his legislation from a "public relations" standpoint even though it would fail.[44]

At the June Senate hearings and behind closed doors, there was considerable support for the reforms.[45] Senator Scott proposed an independent commission which Republicans considered essential so that the disclosed information, now controlled by the Democratic Congress, would not be used against them. After a bill was reported from committee, the Senate rejected two amendments: one by Clark to require congressional members and candidates to disclose outside income and another from Williams to ban all corporate and union spending of funds on political activities. Senators Ted Kennedy (D-Mass.) and Walter Mondale (D-Minn.) defeated the amendment. The Senate bill limited individual contributions, expanded disclosure, and eliminated spending ceilings.

Within the House, Representatives Ashmore and Goodell promoted the ideas that had been rejected the year before. Their Subcommittee on Elections reported a bill in June that expanded reporting requirements to primary elections and to all political committees, created a bipartisan commission, strengthened regulations on political action committees, and eliminated spending ceilings. The AFL-CIO warned that the definition of "committee" was so broad it would include spending on political education. AFL-CIO lobbyist Andrew Biemiller felt that the union needed to obtain language that would "pull the teeth of the bad provisions" and at the same time "look like we're just being boy scouts."[46] The legislation encountered resistance in the full committee from southerners, liberal Democrats, and Republicans. Liberal Democrat Frank Thompson (D-N.J.) fought against provisions on PACs, southerners opposed primary regulations, and Republicans wanted stronger PAC limits. The deadlock ended when the committee abandoned the provisions against labor, which enabled liberal Democrats to support the legislation. Although the House Administration passed the measure, the Rules Committee prevented it from reaching the floor. Thus, despite passage of the Senate bill, the House never voted on any legislation.

Advocates of reform doubted that campaign spending limits would survive constitutional challenge. While the Supreme Court did not review any cases directly and sent mixed messages on this issue, several rulings in the 1950s and 1960s indicated a bias toward protecting speech in elections.[47] In the 1964 decision New York Times Co. v. Sullivan, for example, the Court ruled that the public had to be exposed to a full range of information about public concerns.[48] In Mills v. Alabama (1966), the Court overturned an Alabama action where a newspaper publisher was convicted for publishing an editorial in favor of a candidate on the day of an election. The publication had violated an Alabama statute prohibiting vote solicitation on the day of an election. The Court ruled Alabama had violated the First Amendment and warned against any restrictions on speech during campaigns.[49] In law review articles, Dr. Alexander Meiklejohn spent much of the decade writing about how there should be no restrictions on information reaching voters in times of elections, a key to effective democratic governance.[50]

By the late 1960s, policymakers were considering campaign reform with increased frequency as a result of the publications by campaign finance experts, the cost of campaigns, the evolving financial practices of the major political parties, and a series of scandals. These debates revolved around reforming, not replacing, the candidate-centered election system. The biggest development came with the passage of public finance for presidential elections, although this was quickly dismantled. The reform coalition did not yet have the political support needed to pass and maintain substantive change.

1969–1973: Reform Without Scandal

The political support emerged between 1969 and 1973. Congress passed legislation in 1971 that improved disclosure and limited costs. Just as important, the reform coalition actively monitored the laws after Congress failed to create any independent enforcement mechanisms. The coalition's reports resulted in unprecedented publicity about money in politics, thereby increasing the political incentives for reform. Much of the information released during this period became central to the Watergate investigations. Without the legislation or the reform coalition, the Watergate scandal of 1974 might not have been nearly as severe.

By 1970, before Watergate, citizens were becoming distrustful of political institutions as a result of Vietnam. Political scientist Gary Orren has shown that public trust in the American government began to decline in 1964 and continued to deteriorate ever since then.[51] This political culture made institutional reform seem appealing.

The debate over reform in 1969 began around issues of cost rather than scandal. In 1970, policymakers voiced concerns about increased election costs. A prominent task force study sponsored by the Twentieth Century Fund found that incumbents enjoyed a significant advantage since challengers could not raise the funds needed to manage a successful campaign.[52] Democrats were particularly aware of this cost pressure since the party faced a large deficit. Following their widely publicized study on television costs, the National Committee for an Effective Congress (a political action committee composed of liberals) drafted legislation to enable congressional candidates to purchase airtime at a reduced rate. They also proposed ending the equal-time provision of the Communication Act of 1934. The provision discouraged presidential debates by requiring networks to provide every candidate with an opportunity to participate. Although Congress suspended the requirement in 1960, no debates were held in the election of 1968 and the issue subsided. Network executives supported a suspension.[53] The proposal reemerged in 1969 as part of the general effort to broaden candidate access to television.

Congress took up legislation in 1969 and 1970, beginning with a bill that included free spots for candidates and additional time at reduced rates. Senators Philip Hart (D-Mich.), James Pearson (R-Kan.), and Representative Torbert MacDonald (D-Mass.) introduced a bill based on the recommendations of the National Committee for an Effective Congress.[54] In response, network executives promised to discount rates voluntarily while adamantly opposing free airtime. The Commerce Committee reported a bill that suspended the equal-time provision and limited the rates broadcasters could charge candidates. On April 14, the Senate passed the legislation 58–27 with eight Republicans in favor. Democrats were very aware of how this legislation could change their electoral fortunes. One representative wrote the Speaker that the failure of reform would "hand a big advantage to a well financed Republican candidate" in his state and similar harm to Democrats in "marginal districts."[55] The House bill also guaranteed reduced advertising rates and stronger disclosure regulations.

The conference committee eliminated the most controversial provision: an independent commission. Most Democrats opposed the creation of a commission since it would increase enforcement of the laws. Republicans feared that without a commission Democrats would use information for partisan purposes. Under the existing system, candidates submitted their campaign data to the Clerk of the House and Secretary of Senate, both of whom reported to Democratic leaders. Responding to the powerful network executives, the committee also settled on watered-down cost control through reduced rates. Using these concerns as an excuse for his general opposition to any reform, President Nixon vetoed the legislation on October 12. He claimed that the bill opened more loopholes than it closed and that it fell short of solving all the problems of campaign finance. It also discriminated unfairly against the broadcast media and benefited incumbents.[56] Democrats charged Nixon with sacrificing reform on the alter of partisan interests; reformers equated Nixon's reasoning with "a man who decided not to undergo a much needed appendectomy because the doctor was not prepared to deal with his liver and back problems at the same time."[57]

As Nixon's veto and the Democratic response made clear, partisan interests and divided government added heat to the campaign finance debate. Since his inauguration, Nixon and the Democrats had been locked in a fierce battle. One adviser warned Nixon that this was the first administration in 120 years to "begin with a hostile Congress" and that aggressive liberals were defining the party leadership instead of moderates.[58] Just as Democrats attacked Nixon by focusing on the excessive power of the executive branch, Nixon went after liberal Democrats by highlighting the chronic failures of Congress. The volatile atmosphere lead to an "arms war" of institutional criticism with each side escalating its attack of the other.

Traditionally, campaign finance reform had been promoted by a small coalition of experts, reform legislators, and reporters. Many organizations sympathetic to other process reforms, such as the AFL-CIO, had been much less interested in the issue of campaign finance. But starting in 1970, the coalition gained its own interest group. Johnson's former Secretary of Health, Education, and Welfare John Gardner founded Common Cause, an organization devoted to good government reforms to curtail the power of interest groups and to end corruption. The Common Cause founders believed that interest-group liberalism, which had promised that the struggle between organized interests would balance each other out for the public good, had not worked as planned. It had disempowered individuals who were not connected to interest groups, which were largely unrepresentative even of those they served.[59] For Gardner, campaign finance was needed before any other change was possible. Common Cause brought organizational muscle to the reform coalition. Common Cause claimed more than one hundred thousand members and $1.75 million in contributions by 1971. The members tended to be educated, middle-class professionals, most of whom did little more than contribute money.[60]

Ironically, Common Cause adopted the techniques of sophisticated specialized lobbyists to promote the needs of the "public" and fight interest-group politics: placing advertisements and op-eds in newspapers, bombarding legislators with position papers, and orchestrating "mass" letter-writing campaigns. The organization thus used all the weapons of a traditional interest group, including donations, in the name of reforming government. Democrats had to strike a delicate balance between Common Cause, which insisted on the broadest reforms, and organized labor, which opposed many reforms (such as PAC limitations) since they did not want to risk losing their hard-earned political influence. Another addition was Philip Stern, liberal heir of the Sears Roebuck fortune, who devoted his life to advocacy of institutional reform and founded the Center for the Public Financing of Elections. Director Susan King developed strong ties with other reform groups to lobby Congress.[61] By 1974, there would be eighteen of these groups working on the lobby for campaign reform.[62]

Public-interest groups such as Common Cause shared the Progressive Era fear that corruption was undermining democratic politics.[63] These public-interest reformers were deeply suspicious of political parties and attacked the organizational mechanisms of parties that had traditionally served as intermediaries between voters and elected officials (urban machines, for example).[64] Gardner said that parties were "virtually useless as instruments of the popular will."[65] The National Committee for an Effective Congress believed that it was urgent to "break the southern and city-machine stranglehold on the power structure of the party."[66] Common Cause and allied organizations also chose to influence policy through Washington-based activities rather than building locally based coalitions to support campaign finance reform. Accepting the permanence of the existing framework for electoral politics, the leaders of Common Cause reasoned that if reformers did not employ the tactics of interest groups their campaign would fail.

Common Cause introduced a new tactic in the struggle for campaign reform: the class action lawsuit. On January 11, 1971, it filed a lawsuit in a U.S. District Court against the Democratic and Republican National Committees and the Conservative Party of New York to enjoin them from violating the campaign laws. Common Cause claimed that both parties regularly flouted the 1925 laws. According to this suit, these political parties were creating multiple committees for candidates and spending more on single candidates than the laws allowed. Gardner issued a statement, lamenting: "I find it less easy to excuse the parties, which had they chosen to do so—could long since have joined forces to put an end to the fraud and humbug. They have paid a healthy price for not doing so. A recent Newsweek-Gallup poll of student opinion found political parties rated lowest on a list of American institutions."[67] Common Cause was joined in its suit by the Americans for Democratic Action, the Twentieth Century Fund, and the National Committee for an Effective Congress. Ruling for the interest group, the district court formalized the "right of private enforcement" of campaign finance laws since no strong public commission existed. As a result, groups such as Common Cause gained the right to bring class-action suits against the parties on behalf of voters.[68]

As reformers turned to the courts between 1969 and 1973, the news media extensively reported on corruption. The stories surrounding campaign finance were written by a new generation of professionally trained journalists and editors who had adopted a critical role toward politicians since the mid-1960s. The conflict over civil rights and Vietnam inspired many reporters and editors to challenge politicians. This adversarial relationship meshed with the needs of the print and television media in their fierce competition for dramatic stories.[69] Reporters in both mediums could now draw on a wealth of data from experts in the reform coalition, housed in the Citizen's Research Foundation, Common Cause, and the Center for Public Financing, who produced studies of how parties and candidates received money from vested interests. In turn, the media produced a record number of articles and editorials endorsing reform.[70] Sidney Scheuer, the chairman of the National Committee for an Effective Congress, pointed out to Congress that in 1970 alone "countless newspapers and magazines" had appeared with such "glaring" headlines as "Unseen Fund Raises Financing Lobbyists," "Bank PAC Funds Data Surfaced After Vote," and "Five Political Funds Don't Report Aid." Regardless of whether each story pointed to a clear violation of laws, Scheuer argued, "each instance stokes the fires of public cynicism and the common suspicion of widespread wrong-doing. As a result, the reputation of politics and all politicians suffers."[71]

In addition to reformers and an aggressive media, partisan interests also energized the drive for campaign finance reform. As political scientist Robert Mutch argued, "principle and partisanship" were "inextricably entangled in all of these regulations."[72] By 1971, the Democratic party was aggressively supporting reform.[73] This support had as much to do with raw economic self-interest, if not more so, than ideological motivation. Large donors had shifted their resources toward the Republican party after Nixon took over the presidency and the Democrats fell into disarray. At the same time, Republicans continued to expand their small contributor base by sending personalized letters to targeted individuals requesting small solicitations. Democrats needed to catch up. This is one of the reasons that the Senate housed the strongest proponents of congressional campaign reform. Since senators faced more competitive elections than representatives and needed to finance more media expenditures to cover entire states, they were more concerned about the pressures of campaign finance. There were internal Democratic efforts to revamp private fund-raising. Under the new leadership of Robert Strauss, the Democratic National Committee focused on fund-raising to avoid becoming fiscally irrelevant. In 1972, Strauss inaugurated a telethon that raised $4 million.[74] The party also increased its small contributor base from 16,000 to 45,000.[75] But this was not enough to match the overflowing Republican coffers. Democrats needed new revenue. In blunt language, AFL-CIO lobbyist Andrew Biemiller warned that without publicly financed elections, "the Democratic Party will be in desperate shape" in 1972.[76] Just as partisan interests led Democrats to support public finance, Republicans now sensed that it no longer served their interest to appear as the party of obstruction in the light of increased media attention on the subject. In March, Republican National Committee Chairman Robert Dole told reporters that the president would not repeat his veto of a bill imposing a ceiling on costs.[77] Working with Democrats, moderate Republican Senators Hugh Scott and Charles Mathias proposed legislation to establish a limit for overall costs, media spending ceilings, and improved disclosure.

The Senate passed the regulations by a vote of 88–2 on August 5, removing limitations on private contributions, creating a six-person independent commission, requiring television and radio stations to charge the lowest price possible to candidates, and strengthening disclosure laws. Common Cause had worked behind the scenes successfully to obtain Senator Pearson's amendment for an independent commission (a measure based on language they had drafted).[78] For Common Cause's John Gardner, Congress's decision to eliminate the commission would create the "appearance of reform without the reality."[79] To gain bipartisan support, Common Cause accepted a commission with six members with three from each party.[80] Labor also supported this structure.[81] Controversy formed around Senator Dominick's amendment to prohibit organizations from using dues to support candidates, but labor-backed Democrats defeated the amendment.

When the Senate legislation reached the House, both the Interstate and Foreign Commerce and Administration Committees had jurisdiction over the measure. While the former was sympathetic to moderate reform, Administration was chaired by Wayne Hays (D-Ohio), an avid opponent. Hays was powerful because his committee controlled the allowances for the office expenses of members and chaired another committee that distributed campaign funds. The acerbic Hays displayed little respect for Common Cause or John Gardner. But Hays was not alone in opposing the bill. Another committee member, Bill Frenzel (R-Minn.), said spending limits would help incumbents who had free exposure. Without being able to spend enough money, challengers could not match such visibility.[82] There were strong supporters of reform on the committee, including John Anderson (R-Ill.) and Morris Udall (D-Ariz.). Anderson believed that if the committee did not pass reform before the next election cycle began, partisanship would undermine the effort.[83]

The AFL-CIO feared for the future of its PACs. The Supreme Court was considering a case of union leaders convicted of violating the prohibition of using general fund money for contributions to federal elections. Evidence revealed that the St. Louis Pipefitters Local Union No. 562 maintained a fund between 1949 and 1962 to which union members were required to contribute. In 1963, they converted it to an independent fund and contributions were made voluntary. The jury found the union guilty, since union officers administered the funds. Those officers were paid by the general funds. When the case reached the Supreme Court, the Justice Department raised the stakes by claiming that it was not legal for unions to engage in any political activities, even with voluntary funds.[84] This argument threatened all union political committees.[85]

In January 1972, Congress passed a bill that limited media spending, forced broadcasters to sell reduced-cost advertising, reasserted the right of Congress to regulate primaries (which the Supreme Court had overturned in 1921), strengthened reporting requirements for all campaign committees, legitimated PACs, and deemed contribution limits to be illegitimate. The legislation authorized labor to seek contributions for political funds as long as they were voluntarily donated without any type of physical intimidation or employment threat. To gain administration support, Democrats inserted a sixty-day delay so that it took effect only on April 7, after the New Hampshire, Florida, Illinois, and Wisconsin primaries. Nixon signed the legislation on February 7, realizing that he no longer had support for a veto. In addition, Senate Democrats unexpectedly attached language providing for public financing of presidential elections to tax legislation. Nixon threatened a veto saying the bill was too costly.[86] Ways and Means Chairman Wilbur Mills felt the tax legislation was too important to risk, so he engineered a compromise: taxpayers could allocate money in 1972, but Congress could not distribute funds until 1976. For reformers, this compromise resembled Senate action in 1967, which effectively killed the legislation through postponement.

One immediate effect was to stimulate intense fund-raising before the laws went into effect. Nixon's team led the way as Maurice Stans went on a whirlwind tour to solicit contributors. The press intercepted an administration letter urging donors to make anony-

mous donations before the disclosure laws went into effect.[87] While
a few Democrats voluntarily disclosed information before April 7,
responding to a challenge from Common Cause, presidential candidates Wilbur Mills, Henry Jackson, and Nixon refused. The flurry of
fund-raising during these weeks would become a central issue in the
Watergate investigation.

Since Congress had not created an independent commission to
enforce the laws, the reform coalition took this responsibility upon
themselves. The courts were a key avenue for enforcement. As soon
as Nixon signed the legislation in 1972, Ralph Nader's Public Citizen, the Federation of Homemakers, and the D.C. Consumer's Association filed a lawsuit claiming that the president accepted money
from the milk co-ops in exchange for reversing a decision by the
Department of Agriculture that had lowered milk prices.[88] In a separate action, Public Citizen filed a suit against the Department of
Justice, claiming that the department had not enforced campaign
finance legislation. Public Citizen and the National Committee for
an Effective Congress filed a petition in March 1972 requesting that
the Securities and Exchange Commission force corporations with
"voluntary" committees to disclose fully their transactions. Finally,
Common Cause filed a suit on September 6 charging that the Committee to Reelect the President had violated the 1925 election disclosure laws. The suit was partially settled on November 1, 1972,
with Nixon revealing the sources of $5 million in donations. On
July 24, 1973, the court ruled that Nixon had to disclose the re-
maining donations. The information that emerged from these suits
was soon on the front pages of many newspapers.

Besides the courts, the reform coalition called on its members
to enforce the laws. Starting on March 30, Common Cause launched
a national monitoring project of the 1972 election. The project aimed
to determine how much was being spent and who was contributing.
Common Cause trained more than one thousand volunteers throughout the states to analyze reports. The volunteers established networks in state capitals and near the offices of the major congressmen
who would be the focus of the study.[89] Common Cause leader Fred
Wertheimer said that this was the only way to keep the issue of campaign reform alive without administrative enforcement.[90] He also
believed that Common Cause could establish itself as the major player
on this issue.[91] Based on initial findings, Common Cause filed complaints against 128 Democrats and 98 Republicans. In 1973, the group
released the data through carefully planned encounters with report-

ers.[92] When House Administration Committee Chairman Wayne Hays attempted to subvert the regulations, Common Cause responded. For instance, Common Cause reported that TRW, a large company with major government contracts, maintained an illegal campaign fund solicited from employees. Common Cause filed a suit against TRW, which led the company to end the practice.[93] Without public hearings, Hays's committee repealed the law that allowed this suit by exempting corporate and union contractors from Section 611, the provision that barred voluntary campaign gifts from persons involved with government contracts.[94] Senators, under intense pressure from Common Cause, killed the measure.[95]

Unions rested a little easier following the Supreme Court decision in June 1972, *Pipefitters v. United States*, which protected the right of unions to establish PACs as long as donations were voluntary and maintained in a separate account. The basis of the prohibition against unions and corporations, the Court explained, was that large organizational money corrupted politics. But if the money was voluntarily contributed by individuals, the rationale did not apply. Based on the 1971 legislation and precedents since the 1940s, the Court did not deny unions this right. Union officers, moreover, could administer the funds as long as they were maintained in a separate account. The case legitimated political action committees. In his ominous dissent, Justice Powell warned that this opinion provided a "blueprint" for corporations and unions to flood the political system with contributions without regulation.[96]

Even with this decision, unions were still wary of reform. While the AFL-CIO supported federal subsidies for presidential elections, they wanted a mixed system that included some private contributions because, as one senior counsel wrote, "the opportunity to make contributions to our friends is one which repays us during the course of the legislative and executive processes." Since labor spent most of its money on congressional candidates, they were less concerned with presidential elections.[97] The AFL-CIO was skeptical of contribution limits because unions, which aggregated the funds of many individuals with modest incomes, might be inequitably treated in the same fashion as those from single wealthy contributors.[98]

Watergate, the scandal that was riveting national attention by 1973, revolved around rampant campaign corruption. The story broke around the bugging of Democratic national headquarters to obtain information on campaign strategies. Gradually the story expanded to include other campaign abuses, including illicit contributions in

1972. The news emanated from the *Washington Post* within the con-text of a preexisting reform coalition that was seeking to enforce new laws. It also took place in an explosive partisan environment pitting the Democratic Congress against a Republican president, each fighting to curtail the power of the other.

Congress, the courts, and the media furthered this effort to make the existing campaign laws effective through the Watergate investi-gations. The Select Committee on Presidential Campaign Activi-ties, chaired by Senator Sam Ervin (D-N.C.), conducted highly rated televised hearings on the 1972 presidential campaign. The hearings focused both on the break-in at the Watergate and the subversion of campaign laws.[99] The hearings, which introduced many Americans to the corrupt campaign practices of the administration, were filled with dramatic stories such as an administration official, G. Gordon Liddy, obtaining a briefcase containing $83,000 and the president reversing policies when the milk industry made donations. During the second half of December 1973, the committee examined in great detail the activities of the milk producers during the 1972 cam-paign.[100] Ervin's panel also looked into the campaigns of Mills, McGovern, Muskie, and Humphrey, and found evidence of illicit corporate contributions to their campaigns.[101] Attorney General John Mitchell and Secretary of Commerce Maurice Stans were indicted on campaign charges. The prosecution presented evidence that these officials had secretly accepted union contributions in exchange for stopping Justice Department investigations.

More Republicans began to call for reform. Watergate turned campaign finance into a political liability for Republicans as many Democrats were preparing to use it as a campaign issue. As one Demo-crat told colleagues: "It is very possible you will find that if you are against public financing you might be accused of being in favor of what has just happened in Watergate; in other words, it may be the most popular thing right now for everybody to be in favor of public financing rather than to think that you are being accused of want-ing a slush fund."[102] To separate themselves from the scandal, Re-publicans stressed that Watergate was the product of a corrupt system, not a corrupt individual or party. William Brock (R-Tenn.), chair-man of the Republican Senatorial Campaign Committee, called for stronger disclosure laws, contribution limits, and stronger restraints on campaign costs. He also wanted to require candidates to desig-nate a single financial institution to hold their funds. The bank would publish the names and Social Security numbers of contributors.[103]

Nixon even called for a nonpartisan commission.[104] Few took him seriously. Charles Colson, former special assistant to the president, published a piece in the *New York Times* which argued that public financing and complete financial disclosure were essential for the nation to move beyond Watergate.[105] However, most Republicans still opposed public finance on the grounds that it was unconstitutional and costly and that it protected incumbents. Even with Watergate, Republicans had less need for public money and did not want Democrats to benefit from new public funds.

By 1973, most congressional Democrats agreed on the need for public subsidies, contribution and spending limits, and an independent commission. Yet there were still important divisions within the party. One disagreement revolved around the relationship between Watergate and reform. Some Democrats, such as Senator Joseph Biden (D-R.I.), wanted to target Nixon, while others, such as Senator John Pastore (D-R.I.), stressed the need to keep the issue bipartisan. A second division was over whether to call for public financing in congressional or just presidential elections. Pastore and others warned of the need to limit the reforms in terms of cost and coverage, or risk losing support. Likewise, Long believed that public financing for congressional elections, based on his experience in 1966, would be seen as a subsidy for incumbents while public finance for presidential elections could pass: "You ought to start right out with the Presidency where the people can understand it. That is where we have already acted and where we have already managed to put something on the statute books and the public has come to accept it."[106] A few Democrats such as Representative James O'Hara (D-Mich.) argued that campaign finance had to be completely subsidized by the federal government. Even a matching funds system, he said, left open the door for corruption.[107]

In July 1973, the Senate Rules and Administration Committee reported legislation limiting campaign spending, restricting contributions, repealing the equal-time provision, and creating an independent commission to regulate elections. Support for a commission had become much stronger as the abuses of the Department of Justice under Nixon became clear. Watergate had made it much more difficult to contend that members of the administration could uphold the laws. The complete ineffectiveness of federal controls on campaign costs, Director of the General Accounting Office Philip Hughes claimed, showed that stronger machinery was needed.[108] While the Senate rejected public subsidies for presidential elections, it did so by an extremely narrow vote. In the House, Anderson and Udall received more support for public finance than ever before but were unsuccessful getting it through committee. When a bipartisan coalition of senators attached a rider for publicly financed elections to legislation, they were forced to drop the measure as a result of Senator James Allen's (D-Ala.) filibuster.

The years between 1969 and 1973 witnessed an increase in the momentum for reforming the candidate-centered system even before Watergate exploded. Congress passed legislation in 1971, which the reform coalition used to expose election corruption. There was now a sense that reform could work. Senator Claiborne Pell (D-R.I.) told fellow Democratic Senators that the 1971 bill "is a pretty darn good law, because a lot of things exposed in the Watergate would not have come up if it hadn't been for the present law."[109] More than forty states adopted reforms before the federal legislation of 1974.[110] None of the reforms resulted automatically from scandal, but from a reform coalition actively pursuing change and responding to policy windows as they emerged.

1974: Watergate

Watergate offered a "focusing event" for the coalition to push their proposals that had incubated over many years. When the press publicized Nixon's misdeeds, there was a reform coalition inside and outside Congress prepared to move forward with legislation. As Senator Joseph Biden (D-Del.) explained in 1973: "Watergate isn't the question. Watergate is merely a vehicle through which we can get through what we originally could not get through because the fellows on the other team are in a very compromising position as a consequence of it."[111] Without the reform coalition, the Watergate scandal might have produced less legislation and the scandal itself might not have been as dramatic. But without a scandal as shocking as Watergate, the coalition might not have been able to secure legislative support for reform.

Conservative organizations continued to oppose federal subsidies for elections. While supporting some reforms, the Chamber of Commerce warned that public subsidies would control "political freedom" by requiring spending limits. Calling for the government to limit private contributions and to distribute public contributions to all candidates equally, they said, was the "height of arrogance."[112]

The American Enterprise Institute, a conservative think tank, published a report that claimed private money appropriately weeded out unpopular candidates. Since most citizens did not have the energy for other types of political activity, moreover, private contributions were an integral method of political participation. It seemed hypocritical, the report added, for Common Cause to contribute funds yet deny that same right to others.[113] Amid public outrage at the activities of President Nixon and his staff, an IRS study found that only four percent of taxpayers had used the opportunity in 1972 to earmark a dollar for elections and fourteen percent in 1973.[114]

Even the Democratic party, which was now aggressive in the pursuit for reform, still needed money. Under the direction of Lloyd Bentsen (D-Tex.), the Democratic Senatorial Campaign Committee promoted its new private fund-raising techniques. The committee organized a $500-a-plate dinner that raised one million dollars for senatorial candidates. The committee also sent experts to teach candidates effective fund-raising techniques. Bensten encouraged colleagues to lean harder on interest groups, who were reluctant to contribute in light of the negative press coverage of campaign finance in the Watergate scandal. The committee also tried to broaden its small contributor base through direct mail, targeting those who had written senators about Nixon's impeachment and resignation.[115]

Notwithstanding these fund-raising activities, most Democratic leaders perceived campaign finance as a defining issue in 1974.[116] Public-opinion polls confirmed that Watergate had heightened public interest in taking action against campaign corruption. Americans now ranked government corruption as one of the most important problems. Of those polled, 65 percent said that they favored the use of public funding in presidential and congressional elections. Support was high regardless of educational backgrounds or party affiliation. That figure had risen from 58 percent between June and October 1973. Seventy-four percent of those polled said that they would like the 1971 federal disclosure laws applied to their state.[117]

The Senate passed a bill that mandated public funds for all federal elections and created an independent commission. Nixon could no longer afford to oppose these legislators as Congress deliberated his impeachment. Several weeks after Nixon's key fund-raiser pleaded guilty to managing illegal contributions, the president called for an independent commission, stronger disclosure laws, rules against "dirty tricks," and strict reporting requirements for PACs.[118] Critics were angry that he refused to endorse publicly financed elections.[119] Senate Minority Leader Hugh Scott had reversed his position because of Watergate by supporting publicly financed presidential elections. Ardent campaign finance opponent Senator James Allen mounted another filibuster hoping to stop the bill or at least to water it down. Common Cause, along with Senators Ted Kennedy and Scott, lobbied for cloture. The Senate ended the filibuster and passed legislation on April 11 by 53–32. The bill included public financing for congressional and presidential elections, an independent commission, contribution and spending limits, and a repeal of the equal-time provision.

The Senate legislation reached the House, where Wayne Hays, sensing that federal subsidies for presidential elections were inevitable, focused on preventing public subsidies in congressional elections.[120] Consequently, Hays's committee reported legislation that included public financing for presidential, but not congressional, elections. John Brademas (D-Ind.), who supported the provision for congressional elections, brokered that compromise. Anderson and Udall vowed to fight for an amendment to extend public finance to congressional campaigns. Frenzel, along with other Republicans, attacked public financing and the lack of a commission in the bill. While the committee was deliberating, the Senate Watergate Committee released its final 2,217-page report. Although Sam Ervin's committee opposed public financing on the grounds that it was a serious threat to constitutional rights, most of the publicity surrounding this report centered on its lurid evidence of campaign corruption. Other developments surrounding this investigation generated momentum for reform. Former Secretary of Treasury John Connally was indicted for accepting a bribe from the milk industry. Criminal information filed against the Associated Milk Producers, Inc., revealed its donations to Democratic presidential candidates Mills, Humphrey, and Muskie.

The legislation passed by the House created two regulatory systems: public financing would attempt to constrain private contributions in presidential elections, while strict contribution limitations would achieve the same goal in Congress. After rejecting an amendment for publicly financed congressional elections and accepting one for an independent commission, the House passed the legislation on August 8 by a vote of 355–48, hours before President Nixon resigned from office. The bill included contribution and spending limits, publicly financed presidential elections, and a part-time independent commission.

As late as August 21, key advisers to President Gerald Ford believed there was a possibility that Hays would block the legislation in conference committee, where the House and Senate had to settle their differences.[121] Hays still wanted to stop the bill, which he felt he had been forced to pass, but he needed someone else to take the blame.[122] The bills went to conference with public finance for congressional elections (which was in the Senate but not the House bill) and the strength of the independent commission (stronger in the Senate than the House bill) the two unresolved issues. Enough Democrats were willing to abandon public financing for congressional elections to obtain the other reforms. John Gardner predicted support for further reform once citizens saw how the program operated in presidential elections. Others in Congress were interested in reforming the presidency but not themselves. In conference, the House accepted a stronger commission in exchange for dropping the Senate's publicly financed congressional elections. Spending limits were set low so that incumbents felt they would help defeat challengers.[123] The Senate passed the bill 60–16 and the House by 365–24.

The final legislation established contribution and spending limits, public financing for presidential elections, and an independent election commission. The legislation did not impose any serious restriction on PACs and even permitted corporations with government contracts to establish these committees.[124] Candidates could not spend more than $50,000 from their personal funds. Independent expenditures, those made on behalf of a candidate but not in any way solicited or connected to his or her campaign committee, were limited to $1,000 a year. The FEC was given the power to conduct investigations, initiate civil actions, and refer criminal violations to the Attorney General. The House, Senate, and President would each nominate commissioners. Congress retained the power to veto regulations.

Although the legislation did not provide public financing for congressional elections, reformers claimed victory. John Gardner told reporters that while this was only a "half loaf" it was a "great half loaf." He explained that this legislation bought Congress two years before they would be forced, because of the inconsistency in the two election systems, to reform themselves. Frenzel called the bill a "hoax." Low spending caps and contribution limits, he said, would turn this bill into a boon for incumbents without doing anything about campaign abuses.[125] Common Cause acknowledged that House election challengers had difficulty raising funds. But the reformers were convinced that incumbents raised more money from interest groups than challengers, so public financing would make elections more competitive.[126] President Ford opposed the legislation but realized that he had little choice but to sign it. A veto was now politically dangerous and Congress might override it.[127] On October 15, Ford hesitantly signed the bill.[128]

The following month, Democrats swept the congressional elections in one of the worst showings for Republicans since the New Deal. The victories were a partial vindication for reformers. Although Democrats generally refrained from using Watergate directly, many candidates discussed the "integrity" issue in their campaigns.[129] Some elections were linked directly to Watergate. In the eighth district of Michigan, Republican Jim Sparling lost because Nixon had strongly supported him during an earlier election. Sparling acknowledged that the "taint" of Watergate had defeated him. Five Republican members of the House Judiciary Committee who supported Nixon were defeated. Senator Robert Dole, who had chaired the Republican National Committee, survived an unexpectedly close race with a sharp reduction in the number of votes he received. Dole said that the "wreckage of Watergate" and Ford's pardon made it difficult for Republicans that year. He thought he would lose.[130]

The election dampened enthusiasm among congressional Democrats, who relied more on interest groups than party funds, for public subsidies in congressional elections. Given the importance of economic issues, organized labor spent record amounts on this election, obtaining great success.[131] In a dramatic turn of fortune, Democrats raised more overall money than the Republicans.[132] Some reformers were still optimistic. The previous vote on public financing for congressional elections had been supported by 187 representatives. In November, a Common Cause survey of House candidates found 242 supporting a mixed system of public finance for congressional elections, including 59 Republicans.[133] But reformers soon found themselves protecting what Congress had passed, rather than expanding measures into new arenas.

Into a New Era

By 1982, Common Cause would launch another campaign for campaign reform, this time focusing on PACs. Between 1974 and 1982,

the new regulatory system experienced setbacks. In 1976, the Supreme Court had voided spending limitations and regulations on
independent contributions. The FEC had become an enfeebled commission that had little support from either party. As reformers failed
to extend public financing to congressional elections, interest groups
focused on making donations to candidates through PACs. Equally
important, as this essay makes clear, were critical choices made by
the reform coalition during the incubation period, such as the failure to place PAC regulation at the top of their agenda.

The reforms did not achieve all their objectives. Campaign costs
continued to rise, while wealthy citizens and congressional candidates could spend as much as they wanted on campaigns. The growth
of PACs indicated to many reformers that private interests continued to dominate politics through contributions. Candidates were as
desperately in need of private money as ever before, and PACs are a
bountiful source. By forcing politicians to seek smaller contributions
from a broader base of supporters, moreover, fund-raising became
even more important than in previous decades. Even contribution
limits were undermined by the unregulated donations to parties. Institutional reform was not the magic bullet that reformers had promised. While the many reasons behind distrust in national politics are
beyond the scope of this essay, the new campaign system could only
offer limited results. Changing the election process could not stop
many Americans from hating politics.[134]

Nonetheless, the accomplishments of the reform coalition should
not be discounted. There was a revolution in the disclosure of political information. Until the 1960s, there was little public knowledge about contributions. By 1974, that system had ended. The
United States imposed some of the most stringent disclosure regulations in the world.[135] After 1974, moreover, politicians were forced
to seek smaller contributions from a broad base of donors. No single
entity wielded the singular influence once held by the Rockefeller
or Dupont families.[136] Until 1988, the role of private donations di-
minished in presidential elections. In the end, the reforms created a
more transparent and porous process where single contributors could
no longer dominate the system without public knowledge.

State University of New York at Albany

Notes

1. Minutes of the Senate Democratic Conference, 9 May 1973, MMP, Collection 65: Mansfield–Mike–U.S. Senate, Series XXII: Leadership, Box 91, Folder 1.

2. I would like to thank Professor Alan Brinkley for suggesting that I use this puzzle to frame my analysis.

3. The best historical treatment of campaign finance reform, the only one, comes from political scientist Robert E. Mutch, *Campaigns, Congress, and the Courts: The Making of Federal Campaign Finance Law* (New York, 1988), 191. While his book provides the sole historical overview of this subject, it is unsatisfying for a historian since he organizes the book by topic. Besides its lack of a strong analytic argument, the structure obscures how the various components and factions of reform unfolded over time in relation to each other. By compartmentalizing each area of reform, the book fails to explain satisfactorily the chronology of how this issue unfolded–the major task of the historian. Mutch (see pages 188–89) acknowledges the fact that many reforms were proposed before Watergate, and he presents snapshots of the debates in his scattered topical history, but he does not incorporate this fact into any type of systematic analytical framework for understanding the history of the period. Mutch stresses the centrality of scandal to producing reform legislation, while I emphasize the importance of a reform coalition. Another useful, albeit brief, historical article is Anthony Corrado, "Money and Politics: A History of Federal Campaign Finance Law," in *Campaign Finance Reform: A Sourcebook*, ed. Anthony Corrado, Thomas E. Mann, Daniel Ortiz, Trever Potter, and Frank J. Sorauf (Washington, D.C., 1997), 27–35. Although I take issue with his thesis, the best historical account of campaign finance reform that relies on the unintended consequences argument is Steven M. Gillon's *"That's Not What We Meant To Do": Reform and Its Unintended Consequences in Twentieth-Century America* (New York, 2000), 200–234. The best nonhistorical overviews of campaign finance are Frank J. Sorauf's *Money in American Politics* (Glenview, Ill., 1988) and idem, *Inside Campaign Finance* (New Haven, 1992); Burton D. Sheppard, *Rethinking Congressional Reform: The Reform Roots of the Special Interest Congress* (Cambridge, Mass., 1985); Larry J. Sabato, *PAC Power: Inside the World of Political Action Committees* (New York, 1984); Elizabeth Drew, *Politics and Money: The New Road to Corruption* (New York, 1983).

4. This reform coalition, and its broader efforts to change Congress, is the focus of my book, *The Cost of Democracy* (work-in-progress).

5. By stressing the political self-interest in reform, I differ in some respects with the political science literature that stresses how ideas can overcome interest. See, for example, Martha Derthick and Paul J. Quirk, *The Politics of Deregulation* (Washington, D.C., 1985), and Gary Mucciaroni, *Reversals of Fortune: Public Policy and Private Interests* (Washington, D.C., 1995).

6. On policy incubation, see Nelson W. Polsby, *Political Innovation in America: The Politics of Policy Innovation* (New Haven, 1984), 153–54.

7. Albert Sacks, "Election Contributions and Expenditures: Present Federal Law and Proposals for Change," 15 January 1958, GMA, Department of Legislation, Box 7, File 21.

8. Steven Fraser, *Labor Will Rule: Sidney Hillman and the Rise of American Labor* (New York, 1991), 503–17.

9. These pressures are gleaned from a survey of the social science literature on campaign finance. See, for example, Sorauf, *Money in American Elections*, and *Party Politics in America*, 5th ed. (Boston, 1984); Larry Sabato, *The Rise of Political Consultants: The New Ways of Winning Elections* (New York, 1981); and Nelson W. Polsby, "Money in Presidential Campaigns," *New Federalist Papers: Essays in Defense of the*

Constitution, ed. Alan Brinkley, Nelson W. Polsby, and Kathleen M. Sullivan (New York, 1997), 51–58.

10. Martin H. Redish, "Campaign Spending Laws and the First Amendment," *New York University Law Review* 46 (1971): 900–934.

11. Alan Draper, *A Rope of Sand: The AFL-CIO Committee on Political Education* (New York, 1989).

12. Lawton Chiles, "PAC's: Congress on the Auction Block," in *Funding Federal Political Campaigns: PACs, Corporate Activities and Contributions, and Lobbying Laws* (Washington, D.C., 1986), 275.

13. William H. Jones, "Political Muscle Desire Began Payoffs," *Washington Post*, 4 January 1976, Sunday, section B; Walter Pincus, "Silent Spenders in Politics—They Really Give at the Office," 1971, GMA, Department of Legislation, Box 7, Folder 20.

14. Edwin M. Epstein, *Corporations, Contributions, and Political Campaigns: Federal Regulation in Perspective* (Berkeley, 1968), 74.

15. George Riley to George Meany, 8 October 1956, GMA, Department of Legislation, Box 32, Folder 23; George Meany, "The Lobby Probe," *The AFL-CIO American Federationist* 63 (April 1956): 16–17.

16. Walter Reuther to George Meany, 5 August 1959, GMA, Department of Legislation, Box 10, Folder 27.

17. William Vanderbilt to Members of the Committee on Campaign Expenditures, 12 June 1958, GMA, Department of Legislation, Box 7, File 21.

18. Jim McDevitt to George Meany, 8 May 1958, GMA, Department of Legislation, Box 7, Folder 21.

19. Committee on Campaign Contributions and Expenditures to Senators and Representatives in Congress, 4 November 1958, GMA, Department of Legislation, Box 7, File 21.

20. Herbert Alexander, interview with Julian Zelizer, Washington, D.C., 4 March 1999.

21. Citizen's Research Foundation, *Financing the 1960 Election* (Princeton, 1961).

22. Office of the White House Press Secretary, Press Release, 4 October 1961, JFKL, Presidential Office Files, Box 93.

23. President's Commission on Campaign Costs, *Financing Presidential Campaigns*, April 1962, JFKL, Presidential Office Files, Box 93.

24. Harold Reis, Memorandum, 3 July 1962, and Alexander Heard to Lee White, 13 July 1962, in JFKL, White House Central Files, Box 206.

25. Robert J. Rosthal to Fred Vinson, 26 July 1965, LBJL, Office Files of Matthew Nimetz, Box 3, File: Financing Political Campaigns.

26. Herbert E. Alexander, *Money in Politics* (Washington, D.C., 1972), 33.

27. Terry Robards, "Election Funds May Set Record," *New York Times*, 31 March 1968.

28. "Campaign Spending Regulation: Failure of the First Step," *Harvard Journal of Legislation* 8 (1971): 642.

29. Godfrey Hodgson, *The World Turned Right Side Up: A History of the Conservative Ascendancy in America* (Boston, 1996).

30. Democratic National Committee, "Financial Report," 25 March 1965, LBJL, Files of Marvin Watson, Box 19, File: DNC/Financial Reports.

31. Democratic National Committee, Financial Records, 1965 and 1966, LBJL, Files of Marvin Watson, Box 19, File: DNC/Financial Reports.

32. Julian E. Zelizer, "The Constructive Generation: Thinking about Congress in the 1960s," *Mid-America* 81 (1999): 265–98, and idem "Bridging State and Society: The Origins of 1970s Congressional Reform," *Social Science History* 12 (2000): 379–90.

33. Arthur Krim to Marvin Watson, 2 November 1967, LBJL, Files of Marvin Watson, Box 19, File: DNC/Financial Reports.

34. Marvin Watson to President Johnson, 25 January 1967, LBJL, Files of Marvin Watson, Box 19, File: DNC/Financial Reports; John Criswell to William White, 16 November 1967, LBJL, Files of Marvin Watson, Box 19, File: DNC/Financial Reports.

35. George H. Gallup, *The Gallup Poll: Public Opinion 1935–1971: Volume Three* (New York, 1972), 2070; 2116–17; George H. Gallup, *The Gallup Poll: Public Opinion 1935–1971: Volume Two* (New York, 1972), 1391, 1445.

36. David Adamy and George Agree, "Election Campaign Financing: The 1974 Reforms," *Political Science Quarterly* 90, no. 2 (Summer 1975): 206.

37. John P. Pomfret, "Johnson Urges Strict New Law on Election Gifts," *New York Times,* 7 May 1966.

38. "Position of Various Senators on Political Campaign Problems," 1967, LBJL, Office Files of John E. Robson and Stanford G. Ross, Box 15, File: Political Process.

39. Richard Neustadt to the President, 20 December 1966, LBJL, Task Force Reports, Box 3, File: 1966 Task Force on Campaign Financing.

40. Record of Meeting, 22 October 1966, LBJL, Task Force Reports, Box 3, File: 1966 Task Force on Campaign Financing.

41. "Testimony of Senator Robert F. Kennedy On Campaign Financing," 6 June 1967, LBJL, Office Files of John Robson and Stanford Ross, Box 15, File: Political Process.

42. Memorandum of a Telephone Conversation, 2 December 1966, LBJL, Task Force Reports, Box 3, File: 1966 Task Force on Campaign Financing.

43. Joseph Califano to President Johnson, 1967, LBJL, White House Aide Files: Papers of Joseph Califano, Box 57, File: Political Process.

44. Joseph Califano to President Johnson, 23 May 1967, LBJL, White House Aide Files: Papers of Joseph Califano, Box 57, File: Political Process.

45. Joseph Barr to President Johnson, 10 June 1967, LBJL, White House Aide Files: Papers of Joseph Califano, Box 57, File: Political Process.

46. Andrew Biemiller to Tom Harris, 29 June 1967, GMA, Department of Legislation, Box 7, Folder 20.

47. Lucas A. Powe Jr., *The Warren Court and American Politics* (Cambridge, Mass., 2000), 303–35.

48. *New York Times Co. v Sullivan,* 376 U.S. 254 (1964).

49. *Mills v. Alabama,* 384 U.S. 214 (1966).

50. Martin H. Redish, "Campaign Spending Laws and the First Amendment," *New York University Law Review* 46 (1971): 900–934.

51. Gary Orren, "Fall from Grace: The Public's Loss of Faith in Government," in *Why People Don't Trust Government,* ed. Joseph S. Nye Jr., Philip D. Zelikow, and David C. King (Cambridge, Mass., 1997), 80–81.

52. Twentieth Century Fund Task Force on Financing Congressional Campaigns, *Electing Congress: The Financial Dilemma* (New York, 1970).

53. Fred Vinson Jr. to Ramsey Clark, 14 February 1966, LBJL, Office Files of Matthew Nimetz, Box 3, File: Financing Political Campaigns.

54. National Committee for an Effective Congress, July 1969, and Philip Hart and James Pearson to Fred Harris, 5 August 1969, CAC, Fred Harris Papers, Box 279, File 12.

55. James Abourezk to Carl Albert, 22 September 1971, CAC, Carl Albert Legislative Files, Box 147, File 5.

56. U.S. Congress, Senate, Committee on Commerce, Subcommittee on Communications, *Hearings: Federal Election Campaign Act of 1971,* 92d Cong., 1st sess., 2–31 March and 1 April 1971, 146–48.

57. Common Cause, "Making Congress Work," November 1970, CCP, Box 216, File: Open-Up-The-System.

58. Bryce Harlow, Memorandum for the President, 6 October 1969, RNP, White House Central Files, Subject Files FG 31–1: Bryce Harlow, Box 5, Folder 4; Richard Poff, "Diary of White House Leadership Meetings–91st Congress," 7 October 1969, GFL, Robert Hartmann Papers, Box 106, File: White House–Congressional Leadership Meeting 7 October 1969.

59. Report by Tom Mathews, 1971, and "Statement of John W. Gardner Re Common Cause Lawsuit," 11 January 1971, CCP, Box 27, File: Tom Mathews–1971.

60. For the best existing work on Common Cause, see Andrew S. McFarland, *Common Cause: Lobbying in the Public Interest* (Chatham, N.J., 1984), and Lawrence S. Rothenberg, *Linking Citizens to Government: Interest Group Politics at Common Cause* (Cambridge, Mass., 1992).

61. Mutch, *Campaigns, Congress, and Courts*, 46.

62. Adamany and Agree, "Election Campaign Financing," 207.

63. McFarland, *Common Cause: Lobbying in the Public Interest*; Sorauf, *Money in American Politics*, 229.

64. Nelson Polsby, *Consequences of Party Reform* (New York, 1983), 131–56; Byron E. Shafer, *Quiet Revolution: The Struggle for the Democratic Party and the Shaping of Post-Reform Politics* (New York, 1983), 410–13.

65. Nick Thimmesch, "Gardner: Common Cause," *Newsday*, 6 May 1971.

66. Richard E. Cohen, *Rostenkowski: The Pursuit of Power and the End of the Old Politics* (Chicago, 1999), 68.

67. "Statement of John W. Gardner Re Common Cause Lawsuit," 11 January 1971, CCP, Box 27, File: Tom Mathews–1971.

68. Mutch, *Campaigns, Congress, and Courts*, 45.

69. Zelizer, "The Constructive Generation"; Larry J. Sabato, *Feeding Frenzy: How Attack Journalism Has Transformed American Politics* (New York, 1991), 25–26.

70. Numerous examples can be found in U.S. Congress, Senate, Committee on Commerce, Subcommittee on Communications, *Hearings: Federal Election Campaign Act of 1971*, 220–79.

71. U.S. Congress, Senate, Committee on Rules and Administration, Subcommittee on Privileges and Elections, *Hearings: Federal Election Campaign Act of 1971*, 92d Cong., 1st sess., 24–25 May 1971, 92–93.

72. Ibid., 189.

73. Press Release, 23 June 1971, CAC, Box 147, File 91; Democratic Advisory Council, Democratic National Committee, "Report to the DNC Executive Committee," 19 July 1973, DNCP, Box 22, File: Democratic Advisory Council 1973.

74. Robert Strauss to Democratic Senators and Representatives, 13 May 1974, CAC, Tom Steed Collection, Box 62, File: Democratic Party 1 of 2.

75. Lawrence O'Brien to Members and Friends of the Democratic Party, 27 December 1970, CAC, Tom Steed Papers, Box 43, File: Democratic 2 of 3.

76. Andrew Biemiller to Edward Kennedy, 9 June 1971, GMA, Department of Legislation, Box 7, File 20.

77. Warren Weaver Jr., "Nixon Shift Seen on Campaign Bill," *New York Times*, 17 March 1971.

78. Lowell Beck to John Gardner, 21 June 1971, CCP, Box 28, File: Tom Mathews–1971 III.

79. John Gardner to Senator Frank Moss, 27 June 1971, CCP, Box 28, File: Tom Mathews–1971 III.

80. Robert E. Gallamore to John Gardner, 23 July 1971, CCP, Box 28, File: Tom Mathews–1971 III.

81. Larry Gold to Tom Harris, Ken Young, and Mary Zon, 1 June 1973, GMA, Department of Legislation, Box 7, File 20.

82. Bill Frenzel to John Gardner, 7 July 1971, CCP, Box 23, File: 1971.

83. U.S. Congress, House of Representatives, Committee on House Administration, Subcommittee on Elections, *Hearings: To Limit Campaign Expenditures*, 92d Cong., 1st sess., 1971, 28.

84. Al Barkan to George Meany, 11 November 1971, GMA, Office of the President: George Meany Files, Box 95, File: Political Education, 1970–72.

85. "Proceedings of the Tenth Constitutional Convention of the AFL-CIO: Volume II," 18–23 October 1973, GMA, 236.

86. "Statement of Clark MacGregor," 29 November 1971, CAC, Carl Albert Legislative Files, Box 144, Folder 1.

87. Editorial, "Nixon's Responsibility . . ." *New York Times*, 30 March 1972.

88. Democratic Study Group, "The Most Corrupt Administration in History," 13 October 1972, Issue Report No. 13, DSGP, Box 22, File: Issue Report #13.

89. Common Cause, Press Release, "The Federal Election Campaign Act of 1971–Is It the Real Thing, or Only a Sham?" 24 February 1972, CCP, Box 136, File: January–March 1972; Minutes of the Executive Committee Meeting of the Policy Council, 22 October 1971, CCP, Box 30, File: September 1970–January 1972.

90. Minutes, Executive Committee Meeting of the Policy Council," 20 January 1972, CCP, Box 30, File: 13 September 1972.

91. Minutes of the Meeting of the Governing Board of Common Cause, 15 February 1972, CCP, Box 30, File: February–July 1972.

92. Minutes, Governing Board of Common Cause, 28–29 September 1973, CCP, Box 31, Folder: 20 July–November 1973.

93. Jack Conway to Carl Albert, 20 September 1972, CAC, Box 134, File 19.

94. John Gardner, Memorandum, 3 October 1972, CCP, Box 23, Folder 1972.

95. John W. Gardner, "We, The People of the United States and Common Cause: Remarks Delivered to Common Cause Membership Meeting," 1 February 1973, CCP, Box 25, File: Speeches–March 1973.

96. *Pipefitters v. United States* 407 U.S. 385 (1972).

97. Alexander, *Money in Politics*, 171.

98. Larry Gold to Tom Harris, Ken Young, and Mary Zon, 1 June 1973, GMA, Department of Legislation, Box 7, File 20. See also "Alice in Wonderland of Campaign Reform," *Memo from COPE*, 24 June 1974, DSGP, Box 27, File: Unmarked.

99. U.S. Congress, Senate, Select Committee on Presidential Campaign Activities, *Hearings: Presidential Campaign Activities of 1972*, 93d Cong., 1st sess., 17–24 May 1973.

100. Ibid., 14–21 December 1973.

101. Ibid., 5–24 October, 12–19 November, 4 December 1973, and 28 January 1974.

102. "Minutes of the Senate Democratic Conference," 9 May 1973, MMP, Collection 65: Mansfield–Mike–U.S. Senate, Series XXII: Leadership, Box 91, Folder 1.

103. Bill Brock to Carl Albert, 4 May 1973, CAC, Carl Albert Legislative Files, Box 160, Folder 1.

104. The White House, Press Release, 16 May 1973, GFL, Ford Vice Presidential Papers, Box 143, File: Election Reform.

105. Charles W. Colson, "Public Office, Public Funds," *New York Times*, 19 November 1973.

106. "Minutes of the Senate Democratic Conference," 9 May 1973, MMP, Collection 65: Mansfield–Mike–U.S. Senate, Series XXII: Leadership, Box 91, Folder 1.

107. James O'Hara, "Remarks at the St. Clair Rotary Club, St. Clair, Michigan," 13 August 1973, JOP, Box 33, File: Speeches January–August 1973.

108. U.S. Congress, Senate, Committee on Rules and Administration, Subcommittee on Privileges and Elections, *Hearings: Federal Election Reform, 1973*, 93d Cong., 1st sess., 11–12 April and 6–7 June 1973, 66–67.

109. "Minutes of the Senate Democratic Congress," 9 May 1973.

110. Michael J. Malbin and Thomas L. Gais, *The Day After Reform: Sobering Campaign Finance Lessons from the American States* (Albany, 1998), 13–14.

111. "Minutes of the Senate Democratic Conference," 9 May 1973.

112. Arch Booth to Members, 8 February 1974, GMA, Department of Legislation, Box 7, File 20.

113. Ralph K. Winter Jr., *Domestic Affairs Studies: Campaign Financing and Political Freedom* (Washington, D.C., 1978).

114. "GAO Issues 'Q+A' Explanation of $1 Income Tax Check-Off," 14 March 1974, CAC, Carl Albert Legislative Files, Box 188, Folder 10.

115. "Minutes of the Senate Democratic Conference," 30 January 1974, MMP, Collection 65: Mansfield–Mike–U.S. Senate, Series XXII: Leadership, Box 91, Folder 1.

116. "Minutes of the Democratic Conference," 24 January 1974, MMP, Collection 65: Mansfield–Mike–U.S. Senate, Series XXII: Leadership, Box 91, Folder 1.

117. George Gallup, *The Gallup Poll: Public Opinion. 1972–1977 Volume I* (New York, 1978), 146, 186.

118. President Richard Nixon to Speaker Carl Albert, 27 March 1974, RNP, White House Subject Files, FG 34, Box 15, File: 2 of 3.

119. Editorial, "Inadequate Reform," *New York Times*, 11 March 1974; "Pastore Criticizes Nixon Proposals for Vote Reforms," *New York Times*, 16 March 1974.

120. Christopher Lydon, "Hays Opposes Public Subsidies for House and Senate Campaigns in Election Reform Bill," *New York Times*, 28 February 1974.

121. Ken Cole to President Ford, 21 August 1974, GFL, White House Central Files, Box 77, File: PL2.

122. William Timmons, "Meeting with Rep. Hays," 12 September 1974, GFL, William Timmons Files, Box 5, File: Meeting with Representatives + Senators–Briefing Papers September 1974.

123. NBC Nightly News, 17 September 1974, GFL, Weekly News Summary Videos, Tape 1, File: F073.

124. Mutch, *Campaigns, Congress, and Courts*, 164–65.

125. CBS Nightly News, 13 September 1974, GFL, Weekly News Summary Videos, Tape F069B.

126. Minutes, Governing Board of Common Cause, 28–29 September 1973, CCP, Box 31, Folder: 20 July–10 November 1973.

127. William Timmons to President Ford, 9 October 1974, GFL, William Timmons Files, Box 2, File: Campaign Financing Reform Legislation. See also Ken Cole to President Ford, 26 August 1974, GFL, William Timmons Files, Box 2, File: Campaign Financing Reform Legislation.

128. White House, Press Release, 15 October 1974, GFL, Philip Buchen Files, Box 14, File: Federal Election Campaign Act Amendments–1974.

129. Congressional Quarterly, *The 1974 Election Report*, 12 October 1974, 2714.

130. ABC Nightly News, 5 November 1974, GFL, Weekly News Summary, Tape F134.

131. "Labor and A.M.A. Top List in '74 Spending on Politics," *New York Times*, 29 October 1974; David E. Rosenbaum, "Special Interests Donate $8.5 Million So Far in '74," *New York Times*, 1 November 1974; "The 1974 Elections: The New Potential," *AFL-CIO American Federationist* 81, no. 12 (December 1974): 1–5; "Proceedings of the Eleventh Constitutional Convention of the AFL-CIO: Volume II," 2–7 October 1975, GMA, 351–52.

132. David E. Rosenbaum, "Who Is Paying for the Election? People Who Want Something," *New York Times*, 3 November 1974, Sunday, section IV.

133. "Statement by John W. Gardner," 20 November 1974, CCP, Box 216, File: Open-Up-The-System.

134. For an alternative explanation of why Americans continued to hate politics, see E. J. Dionne Jr., *Why Americans Hate Politics* (New York, 1991).

135. Herbert E. Alexander, "Political Finance Regulation in International Perspective," in *Parties, Interest Groups, and Campaign Finance Laws*, ed. Michael J. Malbin (Washington, D.C, 1980), 336.

136. Robert H. Salisbury, "The Paradox of Interest Groups in Washington—More Groups, Less Clout," in *The New American Political System*, ed. Anthony King, 2d ed. (Washington, D.C., 1990), 203–29.

Contributors

PAULA BAKER teaches history at the University of Pittsburgh and is completing *The American Political Industry*, a study of the business of politics.

ROBERT E. MUTCH is the author of *Campaigns, Congress, and Courts: The Making of Federal Campaign Finance Law* (New York, 1988).

MARK WAHLGREN SUMMERS teaches American History at the University of Kentucky and has written several books on nineteenth-century political history. Currently, he is completing *Party Games: The Owners Manual of Gilded Age Politics*.

JULIAN E. ZELIZER is Associate Professor of History and Public Policy at the State University of New York at Albany. He is the author of *Taxing America: Wilbur D. Mills, Congress, and the State, 1945–1975*, winner of the 1988 D. B. Hardeman Prize and the 2000 Ellis Hawley Prize. He is currently working on a history of congressional reform since World War II that will be published by Cambridge University Press.

www.ingramcontent.com/pod-product-compliance
Lightning Source LLC
Chambersburg PA
CBHW021834020426
42334CB00014B/630